I0801275

JOHNSEN SCHMALING ON RIGOR

Photography Credits:

All photography in this book by John J. Macaulay, except:

Page 12: Kevin Miyazaki (The Blatz)

Page 13: Doug Edmunds (Salve Staff Canteen)

Page 17: Bernd Fiedler (Topo House)

Page 163: Sitsrub Ognat (Topo House)

Page 226: Kevin Miyazaki (The Blatz)

Pages 206-225: Justin Lee Lopez (Flex House)

Page 227: Doug Edmunds (Salve Staff Canteen)

Cover Quotes:

Asad Syrkett, "Design Vanguard 2011: Johnsen Schmaling Architects," *Architectural Record,* December 2011, [13], 42-45

S. Claire Conroy, "The Secrets of the Trees," *Residential Design,* Vol. 3, Fall 2017, 17-22

Karl Wallick, "Peripheral Discipline: The Architecture of Johnsen Schmaling," *World Architecture Review,* Vol. 35 No. 192, April 2020, 8-11

Bruce Snider, "Leadership Awards: Johnsen Schmaling's Houses Distill Geometry into Poetry," *Residential Architect,* September/October 2012, [1], 67, 72-77

JOHNSEN SCHMALING ON RIGOR

with an introduction by Clifford Pearson

ORO EDITIONS

CONTENT

ON DELIGHT

By Clifford Pearson

Brian Johnsen and Sebastian Schmaling use words such as "rigorous" and "disciplined" to describe their work. They apply logic and order to every project and eschew big architectural gestures and bold formal moves. Their buildings, many of them located in the coldest parts of the United States, exhibit a Nordic and Germanic sense of reserve, an attitude of principled simplicity and restraint. The work of Johnsen Schmaling Architects does not scream for attention. And yet, the results of all this mental toughness are places of pure delight—country houses that maximize the pleasure of their natural settings, urban homes that entertain the eye with color, even dental clinics washed in daylight. You don't need to be an ascetic or hermit to be drawn to the firm's mountain retreats and cabins tucked in the woods.

Design critics often focus on the exquisite exterior surfaces of Johnsen Schmaling's buildings—the richly patinated rusting steel of the Studio for a Composer, for example, or the multi-colored wood-veneer panels of the Camouflage House—and admire the rectilinear compositions of facade elements beautifully pieced together. Yes, these building envelopes are both pleasing to the eye and intriguing to the mind. But they are preludes to the spaces inside, where people can enjoy carefully framed views of lakes or hills and feel immersed in nature while staying warm and dry. The rigor of the architecture lets you relax and soak in the beauty of the surroundings.

Context drives all of the firm's work, whether it is a sprawling site in the mountains, a suburban lot squeezed between uninspiring neighbors, or a former train yard in a newly emerging part of town. A standard modernist response, especially to naturally beautiful locations, is to create a dramatic contrast between architecture and site—

previous I Camouflage House (2006): approach

below I Camouflage House: photographic record of a shadow box exploring rhythmic shifts between tree trunks and wall planes; conceptual facade model

the lovely white box overlooking a rugged seacoast, for example, or the glass-and-steel pavilion floating above the prairie. The opposite approach is to try to blend in by resting a stone structure on top of a rocky site or draping a building with plants, vines, and grasses.

Johnsen and Schmaling do something harder and more intriguing: they extract the essence of a place, its DNA, and grow a unique design from it. The Camouflage House, a seminal project that put the architects on the map in 2007 and reveals key ideas that still drive their work, doesn't really hide in place, despite its name, but interprets critical characteristics of the woods around it and expresses them in architecture. The cedar and wood-veneer panels wrapping the house don't copy the colors or even the textures of nearby trees, but rather convey the notion of nature. The irregular spacing of glass and wood on the facades isn't a means of disguising the house, but a way of riffing on the syncopated rhythm of light dappling through a forest. Doing this right is akin to practicing alchemy or

below I OS House (2010):
the third-floor study cantilevers over the main building volume; view from the street

other black arts and involves turning base materials—such as inexpensive veneers and engineered wood products—into architectural gold. To Johnsen and Schmaling, fitting in isn't a matter of copying, but of translating what they find.

Sometimes, rooting a building to a place means going way back. As its name implies, the Kettle Moraine House *(p.20)* connects to a geological past. It does this figuratively, not literally—using a long, board-formed concrete wall running along one side of the driveway to allude to the time thousands of years ago when receding glaciers scraped the area's soil. The house itself pushes into the ground to minimize its apparent mass and improve its thermal prformance. The architects also kept the ruins of an old stone barn on the property as a reminder of the vernacular architecture that once dotted the landscape and have restored the prairie that was here before farming began. This project reminds us that history is an ongoing process, not a snapshot.

below I Ferrous House (2008):
facade detail; view from the street

Johnsen Schmaling's urban and suburban projects tap into a more recent past, acknowledging existing buildings from another century, even as they employ a precise contemporary architectural vocabulary. Oak Park Housing *(p.42)*, for example, is an unapologetically modernist ensemble, but it roughly matches the height of neighboring structures, and its polychrome facades pick up colors found on cottages in the area. Meanwhile, the OS House in a historic district in Racine, Wisconsin, eliminates the pitched roofs of its neighbors, but respects their size and abstracts their forms. A projecting upper floor offers a modern interpretation of a nearby gable, simplifying it but capturing the desire to provide a visual punctuation mark. The house looks different, but it fits in.

With the Ferrous House, the architects addressed a classic challenge of the suburbs: what to do with an outdated production house in a typical subdivision. Instead of tearing it down and throwing away all of its materials, Johnsen and Schmaling saved money and embodied energy by reusing the

below I Belay MKE (2017):
facade detail of the weathering steel skin;
at one end of the building, the roof plane folds down
and transforms into a decorative wall

existing foundations, perimeter walls, and plumbing stacks. They transformed the building, though, on the inside and out, creating a house with much more daylight, more storage, and an open interior that accommodates the way people live today. The result is the opposite of a McMansion: it serves as a prototype for a responsibly sized, ecologically correct house that points the suburbs in a new direction.

For Belay MKE, the architects drew from an urban site's history as a train yard, using industrial materials like weathering steel and concrete board that give the 46-unit apartment building an appropriately rugged character. A long expanse of corrugated steel panels hides services and a four-story-high rock-climbing space operated by a local gym. Irregularly spaced vertical slivers of glass between the rusted-steel panels create a sense of motion, as if the horizontal bands of metal were freight trains rolling along tracks that no longer exist. You can almost hear the noise of metal wheels click-click-clicking across the site, a ghost soundtrack conjured from visual cues.

below I The Blatz (2007):
pivoting bottle doors in the lobby;
a suspended canopy guides visitors into the building

Back in Racine, Johnsen and Schmaling designed an art gallery and studio *(p.72)* at the end of a row of historic brick buildings, aiming to rejuvenate a downtown block that had experienced decades of urban decay. The new structure matches the height and floor levels of an adjacent building, making a comfortable fit with the existing streetscape. It also translates the vertical rhythm of its neighbor's second-story windows into a contemporary composition of tall glass panes and slender vertical louvers. Sitting at the end of the block, the gallery and studio building needs to find a way of turning the corner both literally and figuratively. It does this by anchoring the ground floor with large bronze panels set between windows and a white concrete masonry frame, while launching the second-story studio as if it were a glass-and-metal ship emerging into view. By projecting the upper floor forward as a trapezoidal form, the architects push it beyond the property line and acknowledge the oblique angle of the street. The differentiation of upper and lower floors is repeated in the corner details—flush bronze panels

below I Salve Staff Canteen (2009):
deep vitrines frame remnants of the historic building structure;
view of the subterranean dining room

on the ground and splayed metal louvers above. Creating a strong symbiotic relationship with its neighbors, the building both completes an urban composition that had been missing a piece at one end and updates it with a dynamic new spirit.

Regenerating the past was the driving force behind The Blatz, an apartment and office complex occupying the old eponymous brewery on the Milwaukee River. The sprawling 19th-century structure had been converted to residential and commercial uses in the 1980s, but hit hard times again by the start of the 21st century. The developer brought in Johnsen and Schmaling to design a series of interventions that would revive public spaces in the historic project. Extracting the essence of the place, the architects used beer bottles as a building material for large pivoting doors opening ontc a lower-level lounge. Measuring nine by nine feet, each door has a welded aluminum frame holding 1,590 horizontally stacked empty bottles, some of which were Blatz originals found in the basement. With

below | Redaction House (2013):
view of the entry courtyard;
a redacted document serves as the conceptual template
for the building facade

light shining through them, the doors emanate an amber glow that warms the space and gives it a new, place-specific identity.

Johnsen and Schmaling also choreographed a new arrival sequence for the property, designing an elegant canopy that uses thin lighting strips with translucent resin lenses to lead people to a new entry vessel set between existing masonry columns. On the roof, the architects used lighting strips on a steel trellis to define a pair of open-air pavilions. Throughout the project, old and new engage each other in an ingenious conversation between eras, materials, and architectural vocabularies. Although each of the firm's moves here is relatively small in scale, together they show the tremendous impact of incremental change—even on a complex as enormous as this faded Victorian brewery.

A similar challenge faced the architects when they created Salve, a canteen for the staff of the historic Pfister Hotel in Milwaukee. Carved mostly from mechanical space in the basement of the

below I Redaction House: strategically positioned apertures frame unencumbered views of the lake

Romanesque Revival building, the 960-square-foot project contrasts a sleek new interior with peeks at unglamorous parts of the 128-year-old structure. Johnsen and Schmaling cut openings in subterranean walls to reveal the forgotten guts of the building—corroded pipes, stone foundations, rough bricks. By framing these views and placing them behind glass panels, the designers treated the past, even the rugged bits of it, as a buried treasure that make us richer today. With its layers of history, Salve reads as an architectural pentimento where vestiges add meaning to the present.

Time, and its passage, are leitmotifs in Johnsen Schmaling's work. In addition to projects that transform or reinvent old structures, the architects address issues of temporality in the materials they use on new buildings. Whether it is the rusting steel shroud of the Studio for a Composer *(p.194)* that is detailed to leave stains on a concrete wall below it, or wood cladding that weathers and changes color over time, aging is seen as an asset, not a liability. This approach complements the firm's interest

below I Mountain House (2015): approach; the entry vestibule offers glimpses into different parts of the house

in surfaces and reveals building envelopes to be skins that gain character as they show the effects of sun, rain, and wind. It also hints at every building's eventual demise, playing on the romantic allure of ruins and the effects of entropy on even the most carefully crafted structures.

The intellectual rigor of Johnsen and Schmaling's work gives the impression that these are architects who play by the rules—of orthogonal geometry, wood-frame construction, 21st-century modernism. But they love to subvert expectations. From the street, the Redaction House seems like a simple assemblage of a wood box resting on top of two brick boxes. One of the lower volumes, though, turns out not to be a box but a pair of perpendicular walls defining an entry court. And some of the long Roman bricks here have been removed, visually undermining the solidity of the walls. Instead of evenly spacing the openings in the walls, the architects make them larger near the street and smaller as you get closer to the house itself, thereby protecting the privacy of the interior. On the back of the

building, Johnsen and Schmaling cut away a portion of the boxy structure to create a covered terrace overlooking a lovely lake—an act of removal similar to the one applied to the brick walls out front, but on a completely different scale. In the house's two-story living space, the architects took a tongue-in-cheek approach to the building envelope, imagining it as a government document with large portions "redacted" or made opaque and the rest kept transparent in glass. Such subversion might actually attract the attention of the FBI, if it were interested in architecture.

Rhythm is a recurring strategy applied to the firm's work, informing the pacing of glass, cedar, and veneer panels on the Camouflage House and the vertical stripes of color on the Redaction House and Oak Park Housing. It influences the staccato placement of thin glass accents on two prominent facades of Belay MKE, animating mostly opaque elevations that might otherwise appear oppressive. It works in three dimensions too, affecting the movement of spaces through and around the Mountain House, for example, and the stacking of volumes at the Redaction House and the Stacked Cabin *(p.108)*. Rhythm lets stoic and rigorous forms dance, reminding us that good architecture is akin to choreography.

Visiting a Johnsen Schmaling building involves moving through a series of cunningly planned experiences—from driveway or sidewalk to entry and living spaces and then to a terrace, a deck, or a patio pushed into the earth and defined by low concrete walls. The architects understand the importance of transitions and the need to ease people from one place to another. Many of their projects offer in-between spaces where visitors are greeted and partially protected before they step inside. At the Redaction House, there's that entry courtyard. At the Pleated House *(p.56)*, a deeply recessed entryway embraces guests with a pair of walls clad in wood—one stained dark red and assembled from stacked timber that moves in and out from the vertical plane, the other made of flush, charred cedar boards. Overhead slats provide shade, while a large glazed aperture on the side offers a view inside and a glass door in front pulls the eye through the house to the woods in the back. It is hard to tell if we are inside or out. Ambiguity is a deliberate part of the experience.

As the firm has matured over the course of almost two decades, it has expanded its reach geographically—to the mountains of Montana and the streets of Sacramento. More important, it has broadened the types of problems it addresses, adding multi-family housing and higher-density projects to its portfolio. But it continues to apply the same intellectual rigor and creative experimentation, which proves to be as valuable in Big Sky country and the changing neighborhoods of urban California as they are in Milwaukee and rural Wisconsin. What some observers originally pegged as a particular strain of architectural regionalism turns out to be a nimble and intelligent approach that need not be constrained to one kind of place or one type of building. I'd love to see Johnsen and Schmaling apply their skills to the design of a public library, a skyscraper, or a major art museum. I bet they would craft exceptional buildings that combine gestural restraint with experiential excitement.

Working from the periphery of the architectural world, Johnsen and Schmaling have successfully honed an architectural identity distinct from design firms in the cultural power centers of New York, Chicago, and Los Angeles. Instead of shouting with grand formal gestures, the architects offer their own perspective, an original voice that articulates a thoughtful, deliberately quiet, and precisely detailed architecture. By arduously eliminating visual noise and avoiding voguish clutter, Brian Johnsen and Sebastian Schmaling have been able to focus on what is truly important—responding to context, respecting ecological imperatives, and serving the needs of the people living in and using their buildings. Doing so, they have created a notable body of work with deep appeal, one that, indeed, delights.

below I Egg Harbor Lodge (2019)

KETTLE MORAINE HOUSE

Campbellsport, Wisconsin

Nestled in the gently rolling landscape of Central Wisconsin, the Kettle Moraine House sits at the far end of an elevated plateau of a recently restored native prairie, its low-slung linear volume overlooking an expansive wetland and small creek beyond. From the nearby country road, the house appears as merely a faint line in the distance, seemingly floating above the grasses and quietly complementing the Kettle Moraine's stretching horizon.

The driveway winds through the prairie and past the ruins of an old barn, a graceful memento of the land's former agricultural use, before aligning with a long, board-formed concrete wall that extends into the site's gentle topography and carefully choreographs the final approach toward the house. An anchor that physically ties the house to the surrounding land, the concrete wall leads visitors to the entry and retains the rising terrain along its back side, allowing the building to partially embed itself in the ground to minimize its visible profile.

The program is organized in a series of three parallel bars, each slightly shifted, split in half, and then pulled apart lengthwise, essentially bisecting the building mass to leave a generously glazed void in the center that serves as the home's open dining and living room. Large-scale lift-slide doors on both sides of the space connect to a long south-facing patio with expansive views of the wetland and the terraced, north-facing entry courtyard that mediates between grade and the elevated prairie plane. The glass entry door, on axis with the long concrete wall and positioned to frame

a small but arresting grove of birches in the distance, leads into a narrow vestibule with a wooden screen wall that separates it from the main living hall. Exposed wood beams articulate a coffered ceiling and extend to the outside as a trellis over the patio; in concert with a deep overhang, the trellis provides ample shade during the hot summer months and carefully modulates the sunlight entering the house throughout the year.

A long, continuous clerestory lines the gym and master bathroom in the sunken portion of the house. At night, the narrow window band radiates its warm light into the distance, subtly evoking the enigmatic clerestory glow of the dairy barns that once dotted the region. The concrete perimeter wall continues eight feet beyond the northwest corner of the house, where it defines the boundaries of a small walled-in garden for meditation and privacy. The restrained exterior material palette—exposed concrete, weathered wood, and glass—echoes the muted hues of the region's vanishing barns and silos. The knotty boards of the precisely detailed rainscreen facade add a degree of rusticity to the overall rigor and formal discipline of the house; they are complemented by a series of randomly spaced vertical stainless-steel rods, their thin, silver lines a subtle nod at the small birch grove beyond. The project included the restoration of more than fifty acres of abandoned farm fields into Wisconsin prairie, rehabilitating the land's original biodiversity and turning it into a new sanctuary for wildlife and birds.

d
c
b
a

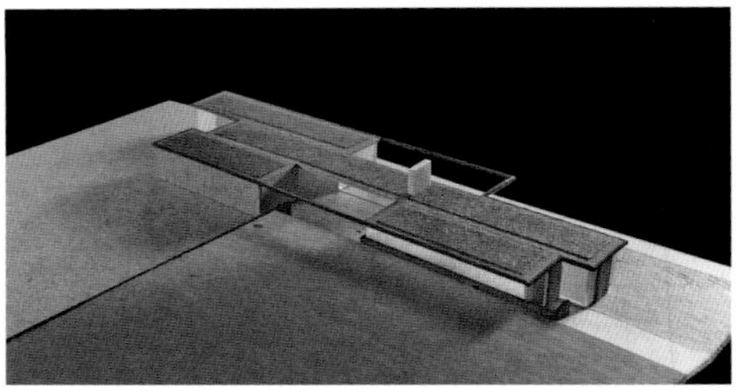

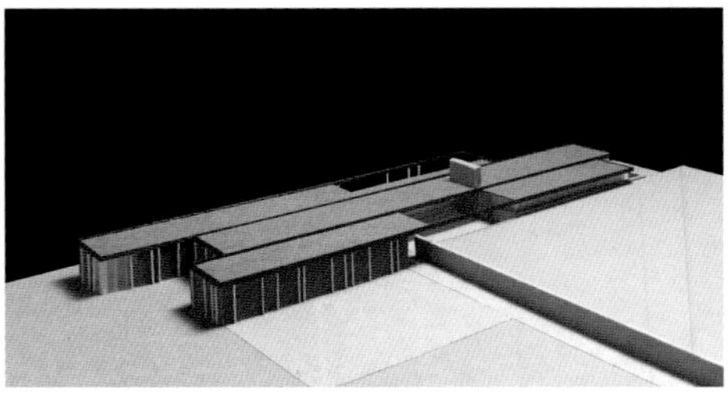

left | a long driveway leading from the country road to the house winds through the restored prairie and passes by the ruins of an old barn

center | massing models

below | approaching the building from the north

drive a.
barn ruins b.
house c.
birch grove d.

right | evening view from the northeast

below | exploded axonometric of principal building components

01 raised prairie plane
02 concrete wall
03 clerestory
04 program bar
05 center void
06 roof plane
07 envelope
08 stainless rods
09 trellis

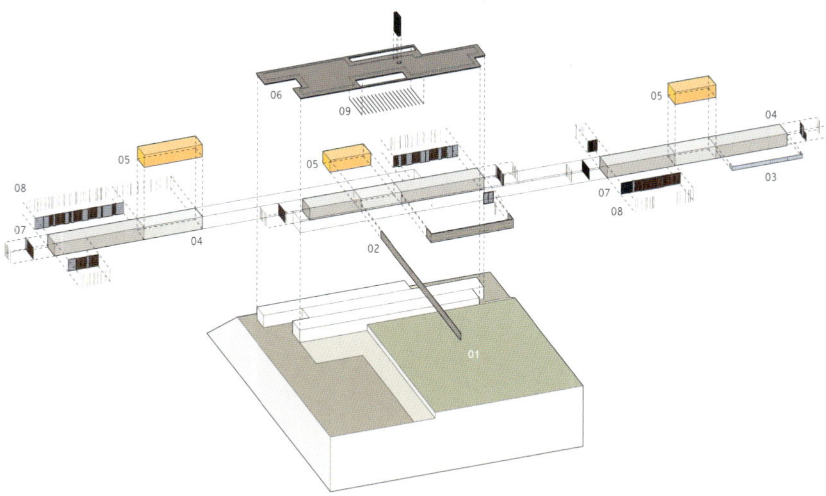

left | a long concrete retaining wall
guides visitors to the entry

below | floor plan and morphological massing model

concrete wall 01
sunken courtyard 02
vestibule 03
kitchen 04
dining 05
living 06
patio 07
piano room 08
bedroom 09
bathroom 10
gym 11
yarn room 12
study 13
laundry 14
garage 15
private garden 16

left | evening view from the bluff edge

below | the living room opens to the trellised patio and overlooks the wetlands beyond

left I on the north side, the living hall connects to the sunken entry courtyard

below I a wooden screen wall anchors the dining area and separates it from the vestibule; a black-oxyde steel cabinet provides storage for wood logs and books

right and below I a wooden trellis above the linear south-facing
patio provides shade and modulates natural light on the inside

left | floor-to-ceiling windows frame expansive views into the surrounding landscape

below | the bathroom is anchored by a custom concrete tub; view of the study

below I the iconic birch grove across the creek informed the building facade: in a reductive design process, the grove (a) was visually distilled to a filigree of white trunks (b) and further abstracted into a sequence of thin white lines (c)

right I the diagram of white lines served as a template for a series of stainless steel rods superimposed over the building skin as an abstract echo of the birches beyond

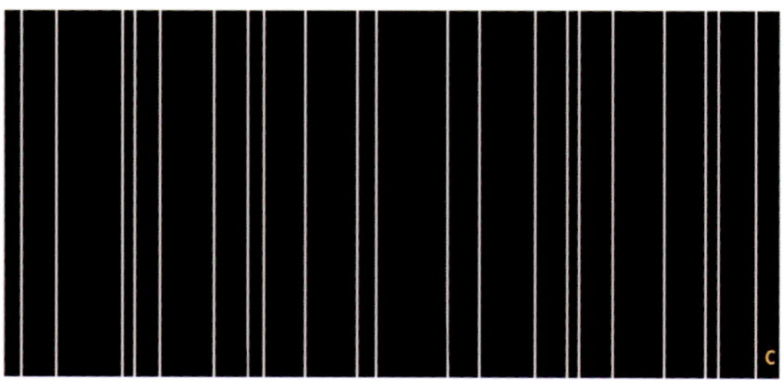

left I view from the kitchen; the slatted wood wall screens the vestibule from the living hall

right I view of the house from the barn ruins

OAK PARK HOUSING

Sacramento, California

Oak Park Housing is a compact urban infill development on a long-vacant lot in Sacramento's Oak Park District, a demographically diverse neighborhood that, for decades, had suffered from economic stagnation and urban disinvestment. In recent years, young professionals, artists, and students have started to revive Oak Park as an affordable community close to downtown Sacramento, with new art galleries, independent coffee shops, and small businesses in tow filling abandoned storefronts throughout the area. This project is one of the neighborhood's first ground-up residential developments since the infamous 1969 Oak Park Riots, which left lasting scars on the city's social and physical landscape; accordingly, the project aspires to be more than just a contemporary addition to the existing housing stock: it is a harbinger of urban revitalization, its architecture cheerfully embracing the creative and buoyant energy that has propelled the ongoing renaissance of this vibrant and socially heterogeneous community.

Designed as prototypical single-family homes around a stringent construction budget to position the homes at the lower end of the market spectrum, the interior program was organized in compact volumes with uncompromising spatial efficiency, avoiding any gratuitous square footage that would balloon the unit size without tangible functional or experiential benefits. Each house has a living area of 1,500 square feet and consists of two simple forms: a ground-level base volume, clad in white poly-ash

3429
3433

siding, and a dark-gray stucco volume that cantilevers over the base to create an overhang along the south-facing front door. Inside, kitchen, living, and dining are consolidated as one open space on the main level, with stairs leading up to three bedrooms that share two baths.

Carefully proportioned to echo the massing and scale of the area's existing building stock, the houses are simple, two-story volumes, their appearance crisp but deliberately playful in a nod to the progressive and artsy spirit permeating Oak Park. Three of the units are grouped along 2nd Avenue, where they repair the fragmented street edge and mend the ragged fabric of the block. The other three homes are accessed from the public alley, continuing Sacramento's unique typology of residential alleys that serve as active neighborhood pathways.

The simple exterior palette includes cementitious stucco and poly-ash cladding, complemented by prudently sized and carefully placed floor-to-ceiling apertures. On the upper levels, the buildings' south facades transform into articulated fields of lacquered vertical metal louvers that act as both sun screen and compositional device. The metered spacing of the louvers sets up a deeply textured, dynamic cadence, their prismatic colors complementing the homes' otherwise neutral, muted tones and cheerfully reverberating the vivid, kaleidoscopic hues of the residential buildings and warehouse murals for which Oak Park is known.

right I view from the street

below I section model and site plan

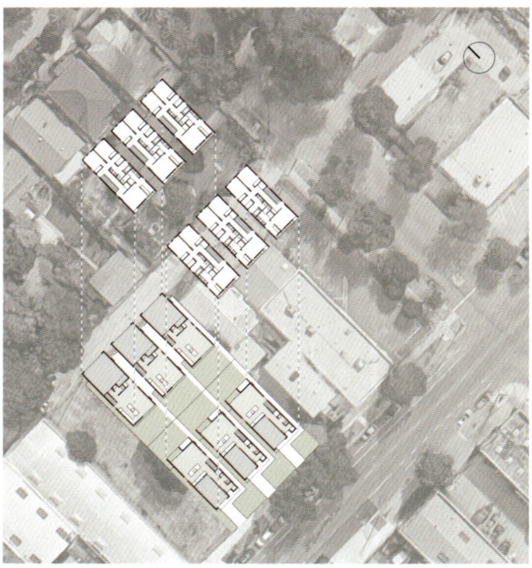

3425
29
3433

below I detail view of the polychrome facade fins

center I color coding of neighborhood homes

right I chromatic sequence for the facade fins

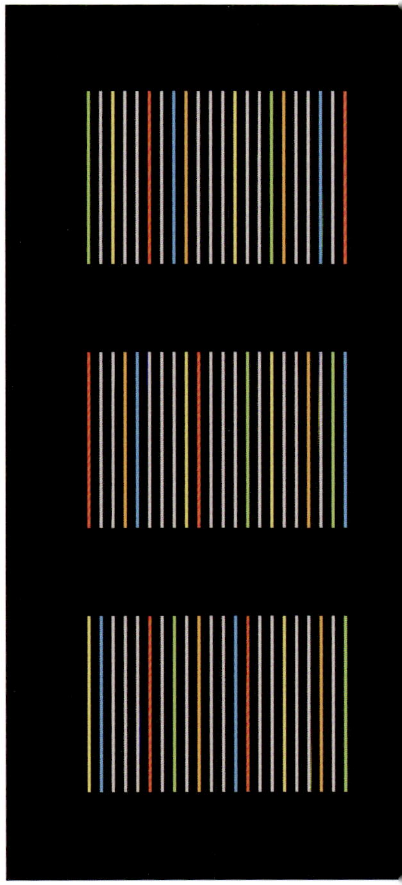

right I the individual building volumes match the scale of the surrounding urban fabric and repair the street edge

below I exploded axonometric of principal building components

01 ground plane
02 concrete slab
03 entry door
04 base volume
05 extruded volume
06 gasket window
07 polychrome louvers

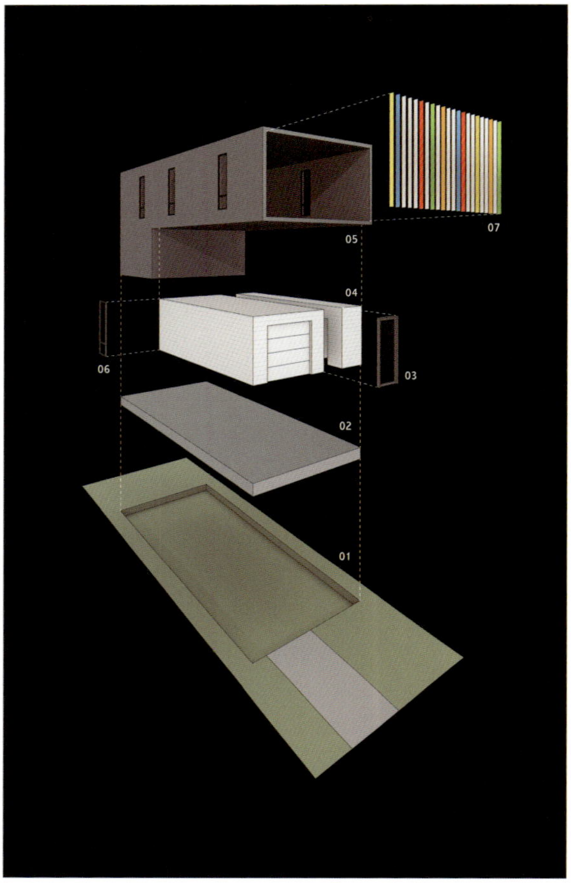

3425

right I view of the open kitchen

below I strategically placed apertures wash the interior spaces with natural light

below I facing the public alley, the homes appear as clean, cubic volumes

right I street view in the evening

PLEATED HOUSE

Door County, Wisconsin

This small house for a graphic designer and her husband sits on the heavily wooded eastern shore of Wisconsin's Door County, a narrow peninsula on Lake Michigan. Embedded in a dense forest of deciduous and coniferous trees, the building's unassuming volume is quietly nestled in a small clearing at the western edge of the gently sloping site, its low-slung silhouette virtually disappearing in the surrounding vegetation.

The building's subdued exterior material palette is dominated by charred cedar siding from Northern Wisconsin, its textured, somber blackness complemented by varnished cedar, dark-anodized aluminum, and glass. Using a century-old finishing process from Japan known as "shou sugi ban," the process of charring is a natural preservative that greatly extends the life of the siding, reliably protecting the material against rod, rain, insects, and fire, all without the use of synthetic sealers or stains.

Echoing the visual depth and surface oscillations of bark covering the trunks of trees, the charred wood boards were installed over furring strips of varying depths to form a gently folding, undulating building skin, not unlike a pleated curtain—a meandering and highly faceted veil that wraps the house and replaces what could have been a conventional, sharply defined perimeter with a more ambiguous boundary, one that softens the building's rigorous geometry and moderates the transition from artificial construct to natural context. A man-made object with an attitude of sincere diffidence to its natural surroundings, the building quietly assimilates with the surrounding forest.

A narrow gravel road leads visitors to a small, trellised forecourt carved deep into the home's rectangular building mass, a tapered space whose forced perspective converges at the glazed vestibule and continues into a recessed covered outdoor room on the opposite side, framing views through the house and into the site's sylvan landscape. A continuous wall of milled lumber, stacked at slight angles and finished with a lustrous varnish to create a highly tactile surface of folding ribbons, extends from the forecourt into the house and visually reinforces the entry sequence.

Inside, the vestibule connects to an open living space with an oversized sliding glass door system that provides access to a linear patio, its paved plane slightly sunken into the existing topography and contained by a long, illuminated concrete bench running parallel to the house. Across from the large sliding doors, a delicate sculptural metal staircase, supported by a filigree of vertical steel rods, anchors the living space and leads to the upper bedroom suite and the expansive vegetated roof covering the main building volume. Contrasting the building's dark exterior shell, the serene interior material palette is limited to white walls, white lacquered millwork, and a gray polished concrete floor.

right I the trapezoidal entry court leads to the glazed vestibule

below I a linear patio runs along the back of the house and connects to a small covered porch outside the entry vestibule

left I large lift-slide doors connect the living hall to the back patio

below I site plan and topographic massing model

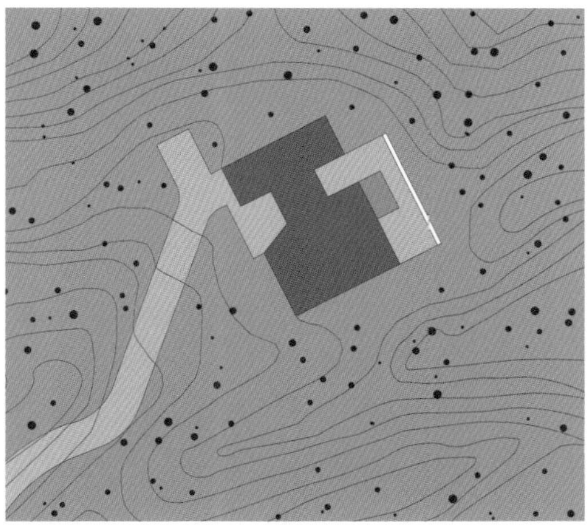

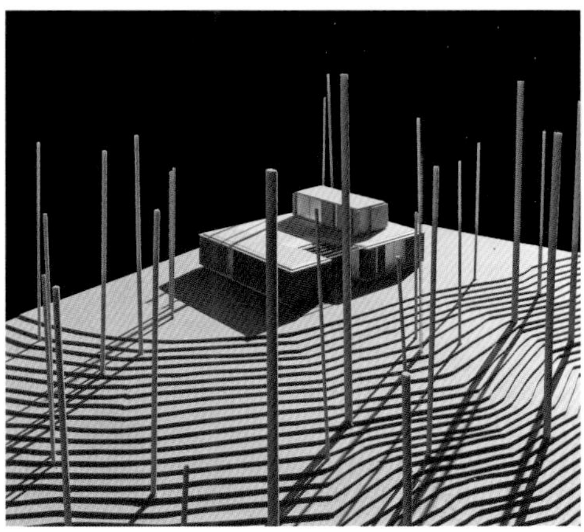

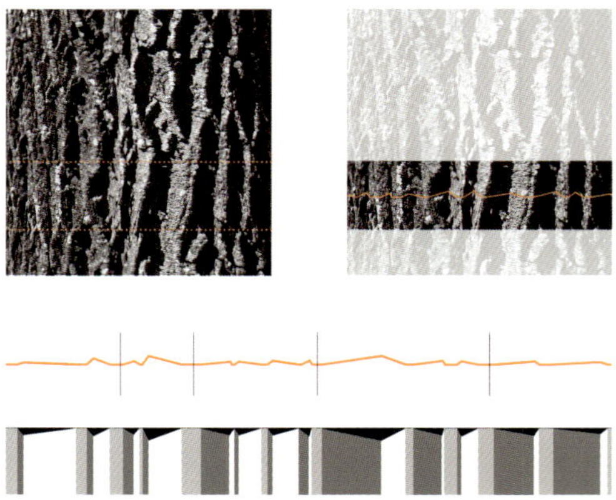

left I the buidling is wrapped in a faceted veil of charred cedar boards

center I the mapping of surface oscillations of bark provided a template for the undulating exterior walls

below I varnished lumber, stacked at different angles, frame the view from the vestibule into the landscape

right I view of the living hall as it spills out onto the patio

below I floor plans and conceptual diagrams

01 entry forecourt
02 stacked timber wall
03 vestibule
04 covered porch
05 kitchen
06 dining
07 rotating fireplace
08 living
09 patio
10 bathroom
11 studio I guest room
12 laundry
13 mechanical room
14 garage
15 bedroom
16 vegetated roof

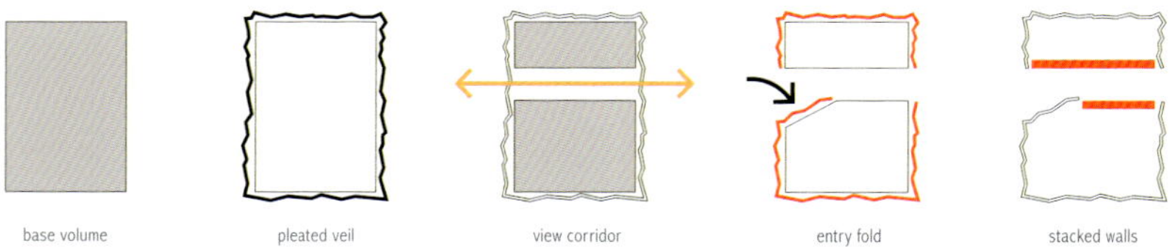

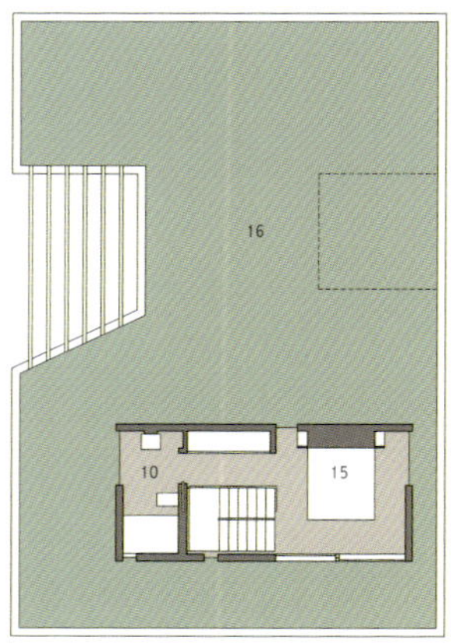

right I the small upper-level volume rests on the vegetated roof plane

below I a delicate steel staircase anchors the living hall and leads upstairs

right and below | views from the back

STOP

ART GALLERY AND STUDIO

Racine, Wisconsin

Located in the heart of Racine, a former rustbelt manufacturing center maimed by half a century of economic struggles and urban decline, the Gallery and Studio building was designed for a painter and local art advocate who set out to create a new cultural anchor for the city, one that would help revitalize Racine's currently anemic downtown. The project pairs the painter's own studio on the upper level with a street-level art gallery; called OS Projects, the gallery is open to the public and features carefully curated exhibits of contemporary artists from the Midwest.

Occupying a narrow sliver of vacant land at the end of a trapezoid city block shaped by two overlapping urban grids, the building caps the block of historic brick structures and re-establishes the street edges along Villa Street as well as Sixth and Seventh Streets, both important thoroughfares that connect Racine's western neighborhoods with Lake Michigan.

While the ground-level footprint traces the orthogonal property lines, an air-rights variance from the City permitted the second floor to partially cantilever over the sidewalk, allowing it to follow the oblique angle of Sixth Street. As the upper level veers away from the building's rectangular base, it forms an acute-angled overhang at the northeast corner that delineates and accentuates the site's distinct urban condition of competing street grids and gives the second-floor art studio a robust street presence.

The building's base volume housing the art gallery features a meticulously detailed white concrete masonry skin that wraps over a field of tall bronze panels and strategically placed gallery windows before extending up as a solid volume anchoring the southeast corner of the art studio. The variegation of the weathering bronze panels is juxtaposed with the material precision and crisp lines of the continuous dark-gray ribbon that articulates the cantilevered studio volume above and frames the 14-foot, 6-inch-tall glass curtain wall enclosure, its mix of transparent, translucent, and spandrel glazing providing the workspace with an abundance of natural light. A series of 10-inch-deep aluminum louvers significantly reduces glare inside and establishes a cadenced field of vertical lines whose appearance changes depending on the sun angle and the direction from which one approaches the facade.

A monumental pivot door serves as the main entry into the building. The door and the wall above are perfectly flush; their matching, brightly colored finishes mark the entry as a vertical threshold that extends from the ground all the way to the top of the building. The top of the continuous concrete ribbon from the upper-level cantilever serves as a small entry canopy before folding down along the side of the neighboring building.

The building exemplifies the transformative role that a small but architecturally ambitious project can play in the reinvention of a struggling urban core. As soon as the structure started taking shape, it sparked renewed interest in a part of town that had laid dormant for years; many abandoned or underutilized buildings and storefronts close-by have since been renovated and put back to use.

BALKAN
RESTAURANT
HOME COOKING
OPEN

right I view from the corner of sixth and villa streets

below I figure/ground plan; urban grid overlay and building shape diagrams; elevated view of the building in its urban context

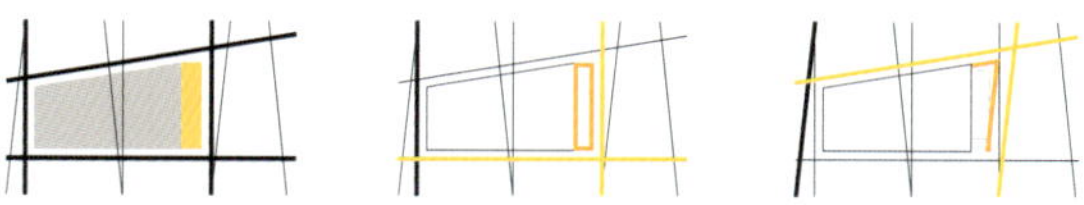

STOP

right and below I the glassy studio veers away from the building's rectangular base and forms an acute-angled overhang at the northeast corner

602

left I view frcm seventh street

below I volumetric evolution; floor plans

vestibule 01
gallery 02
office 03
restroom 04
mechanical 05
storage 06
art studio 07
work island 08
studio patio 09
art storage 10
bathroom 11
kitchenette 12

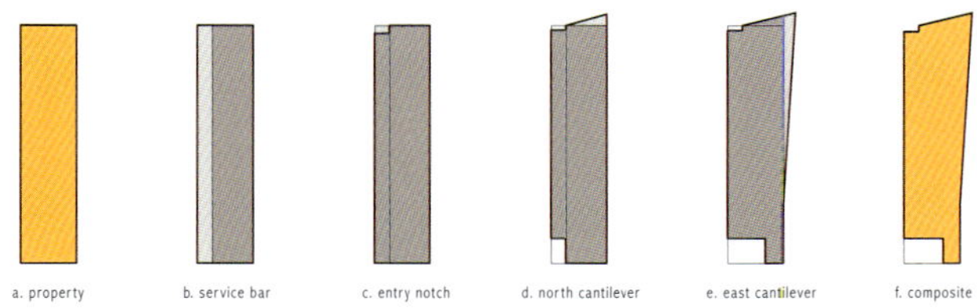

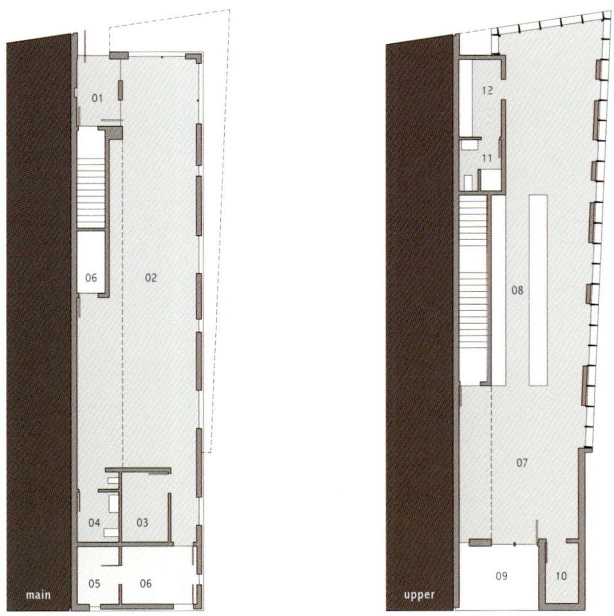

right I the upper studio cantilever traces the site's oblique street grid

below I exploded axonometric of principal building components; model views

01 main entry
02 masonry base
03 gallery apertures
04 bronze panels
05 studio glazing
06 studio ribbon
07 vertical louvers
08 studio patio

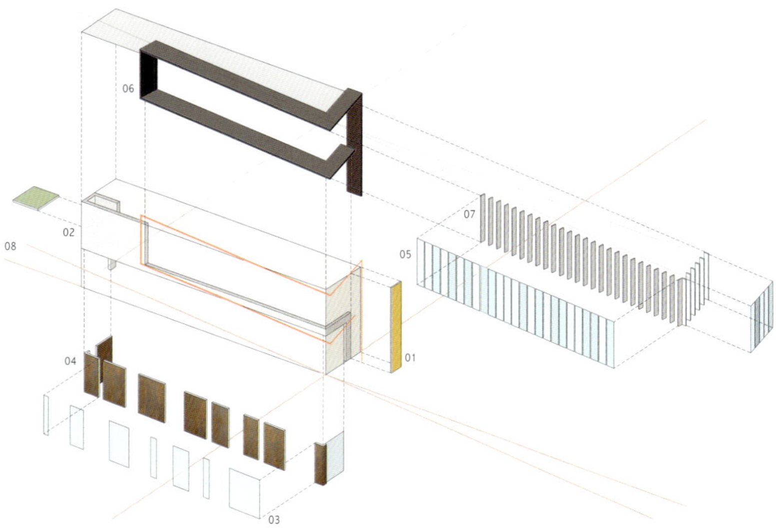

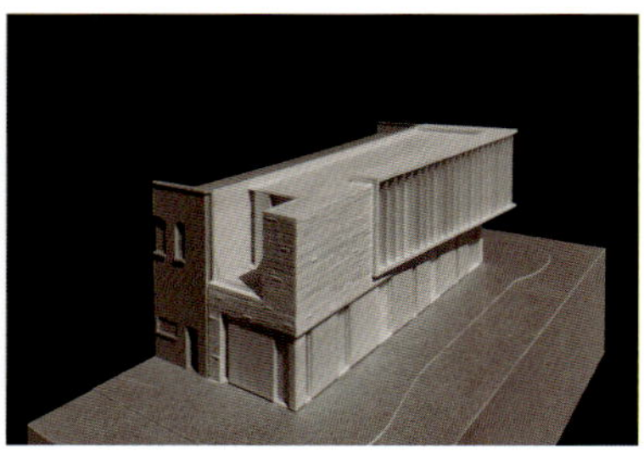

right and below | the street-level public gallery focuses on contemporary art from the midwest and serves as a lively community hub

Seams Appar
MAUREEN FRITCHEN GINA

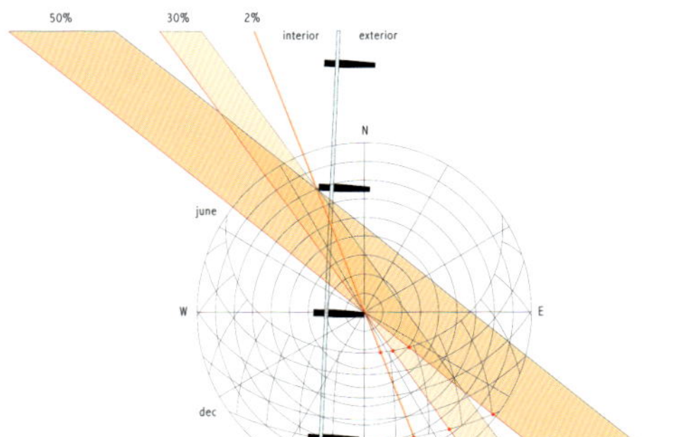
50%
30%
2%
interior
exterior
N
june
W
E
dec
S
june: 11:20AM
dec: 10:30AM
june: 10:45AM
dec: 9:20AM
june: 10:10AM
dec: 8:00AM

left I deep aluminum louvers modulate natural light in the upper level art studio

center I studio facade light penetration study (plan view)

below I custom-fabricated bronze panels complement white masonry and glass

right I the upper level art studio is a tall, vertical space washed in light

below I a long work island anchors the studio

510 HOUSE

Fox Point, Wisconsin

The 510 House is a private residence located in a postwar suburb on Milwaukee's north shore, its volume carefully embedded in the site's gently sloping contours and cradled by the mature trees and thick underbrush that line the property's edges. The owners, a professional couple with busy work schedules, asked for a house that would accommodate their conflicting desires for privacy and serenity on one hand, and for the frequent hosting of social events on the other.

In response, the program of the house was organized as two interlocking building forms, their "T" configuration bifurcating the site into a "public" entry court for visitors and vehicles, and a private, visually shielded greenspace in the back. Parking, service functions, and the main bedroom suite are consolidated in a long, single-story bar, a narrow, wood-clad volume that straddles the two sides of the property along its western edge. Spaces for guests and entertainment are housed in a complementary, perpendicular volume defined by a continuous concrete block ribbon that engages the wood-clad bar, negotiates the dropping topography of the site, and ultimately folds up to form an elevated observatory with views of the surrounding treetops and the shores of Lake Michigan in the near distance.

The deeply recessed entry vestibule, marking the junction of the two interlocking building forms, provides access to both private and public quarters and leads into the adjacent open living hall—the social epicenter of the home where the owners and their guests can cook, dine, and lounge together, all in a commodious space defined by a series of carefully variegated, green-hued perimeter walls. The color green, whose spectral wavelength of 510 nanometers became the project's

namesake, serves as an architectural device to infuse the interior year-round with the lush tones of summer's verdant but short-lived greenery surrounding the site—an abstract and deliberately cheerful echo of nature's chromatic vibrancy, particularly potent during those long, protracted winter months when the actual apertures of the house frame somber views into Wisconsin's frozen landscape. As the seasons turn and the northern winter begins to bleach the surroundings, the walls' immutably vibrant chroma progressively contrasts the changing conditions outside, serving as a quiet memento of the passing of time and a hopeful reminder of nature's impending renewal.

The green perimeter walls extend their interior hues to the exterior, where they express the volume of the living hall as the building's proud *piano nobile*—a distinct and intelligible architectural element suspended within the folding concrete ribbon of the main building mass to formally emphasize the primary activity hub of the house. An open, linear kitchen runs along one side of the living hall. The pantry wall transforms into a wooden ceiling plane that spatially defines the dining and lounging area and folds down at the opposite end to accommodate the built-in media cabinet. A complementary small sitting area faces the kitchen island and is backed by tall sheets of glass that enclose the delicate steel stairs beyond. The stairs lead up to the observatory, which provides access to an expansive vegetated roof, and down to a small guest lounge and bedroom suite, which spills out to an intimate sunken terrace with a fire pit and a low perimeter wall that offers casual seating for larger gatherings.

right I the master suite overlooks the back yard and connects to a private terrace

below I site plan

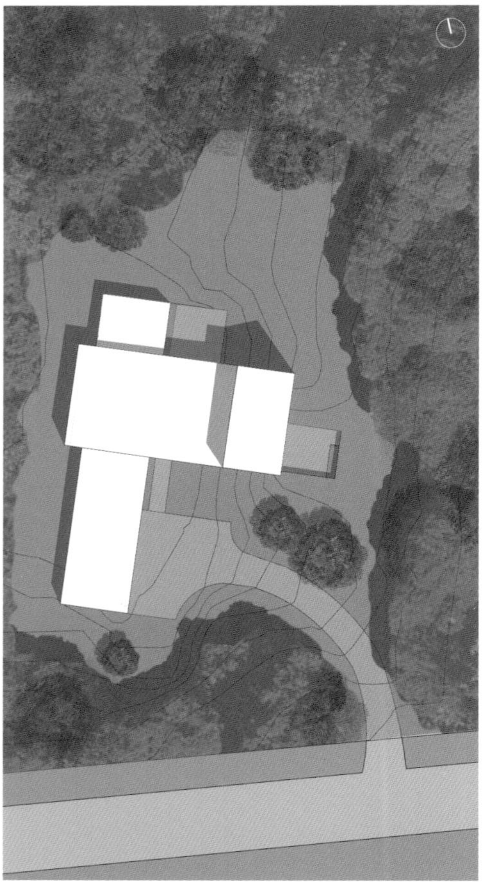

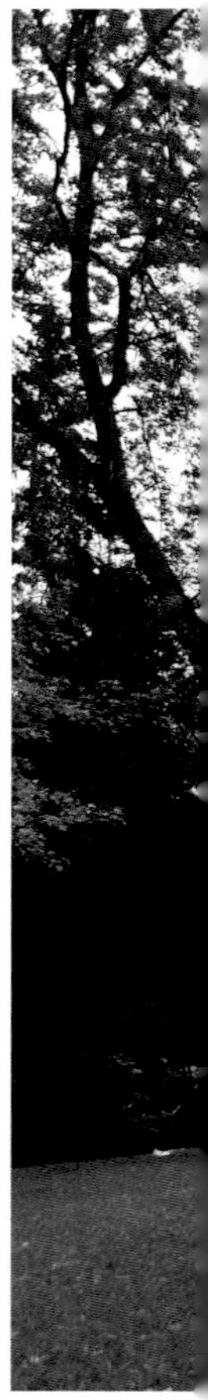

right I a series of wall panels in different shades of green
mark the home's social epicenter as the building's proud *piano nobile*

below I facade concept diagram

right I view from the back yard

center I exploded axonometric

left I building sections; section model

01 ground plane
02 recessed entry
03 service bar: private
04 living hall I piano nobile: public
05 folding concrete ribbon
06 apertures
07 vegetated roof
08 sunken patio

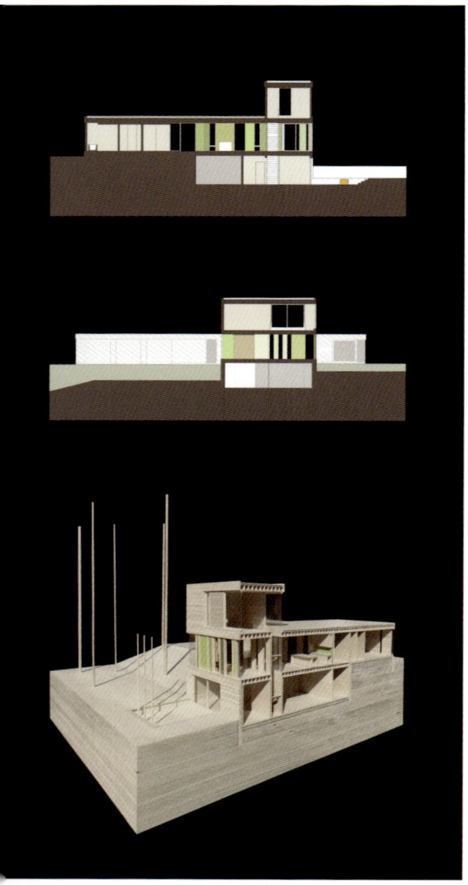

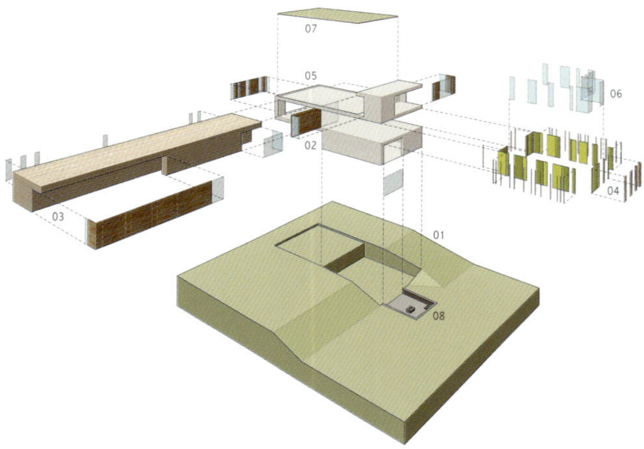

FROST

left I a continuous wood ribbon defines dining and living spaces

below I floor plans

entry 01
kitchen 02
pantry 03
living I dining 04
covered porch 05
powder room 06
bathroom 07
bedroom 08
office I study 09
mud room I laundry 10
garage 11
lounge I guests 12
sunken patio 13
mechanical 14
observatory 15
vegetated roof 16

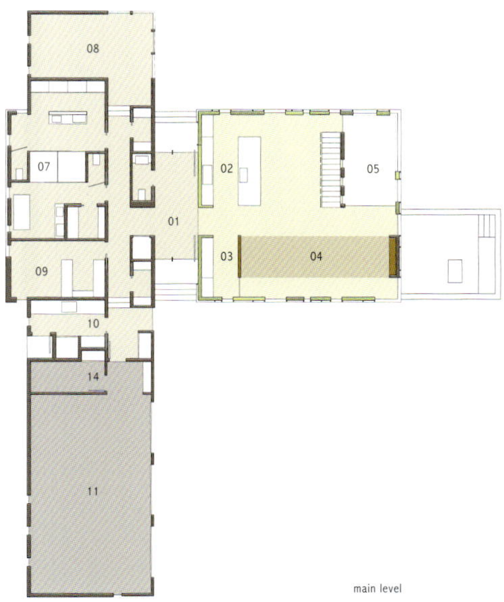

main level

upper level

LOVE UNITES

LOVE UNITES

left I view from the east, where the building appears as a three-story volume with an observatory, covered porch, and sunken courtyard

below I view of the kitchen and living hall

right I view of the sitting area, with steel stairs leading up to the observatory

below I the observatory provides access to the adjacent green roof; view of the sunken patio

right I the concrete block ribbon folds up and cradles the observatory

below I views of the green roof; inside the observatory

STACKED CABIN

Muscoda, Wisconsin

The Stacked Cabin is a modest, 880-square-foot retreat for a young family. Sitting at the end of an old logging road, its compact volume hugs the edge of a small clearing in a remote central Wisconsin forest.

The tight budget demanded a rigorously simple structure. In an effort to minimize the building's footprint and take advantage of the sloped site, the horizontally organized components of a traditional cabin compound—typically an open-plan longhouse with communal living space, an outhouse, and a freestanding toolshed—were reconfigured and stacked vertically.

The bottom level, carved into the hill and accessible from the clearing, houses a small workshop, equipment storage, and a washroom, providing the infrastructural base for the living quarters above. A wood-slatted entry door opens to stairs that lead up to the hearth room, an open living space centered around a wood-burning stove and bracketed by a simple galley kitchen and a pair of small, open sleeping rooms.

Floor-to-ceiling sheer curtains on either end of the living hall can be moved or retracted, their undulating fabric and delicate texture adding a sensual dimension to the crisp interior palette. Depending on their arrangement, the curtains can provide privacy for the sleeping rooms, open them up to the main living space, or screen the kitchen when not in use. Monumental lift-slide apertures along the sides of the living hall offer expansive views of the forest and direct access to an informal hillside terrace. In the summer, the apertures become screened openings, virtually transforming the hearth

room into a covered outdoor space and facilitating a high degree of cross-ventilation that eliminates the need for mechanical conditioning. A small study, originally conceived as another room adjacent to the living hall, was instead stacked on top of it, creating an intimate, elevated observatory of the site—an away-room with treetop views.

The carefully assembled building envelope takes advantage of readily available materials found in the region's farmstead architecture. On the outside, exposed concrete, cedar, anodized metal, and cementitious plaster all echo the quiet, earthy hues of the surrounding forest and nearby rock formations. The material palette extends to the inside, where integrally colored polished concrete floors on the two main levels provide sufficiently durable surfaces against the periodic abuse from cross country skies, dogs, and muddy hiking boots. Walls, ceilings, and built-in cabinets are painted white, lightening up the interiors during the long winter months and providing a quiet, neutral foreground against which nature's complex and ever-changing tableau, carefully framed by the cabin's large openings, can unfold.

Landscaping was kept to a minimum to emphasize the cabin's natural setting. The existing coarse gravel road was maintained, while the natural forest floor was restored around the building perimeter—a highly permeable ground plane that helps minimize the impact of stormwater run-off on the site and allows the building to "grow in" over time.

left I view from the logging road;
the concrete base is carved into the slope of the site

below top I the facade openings increase from base to roof, analogous to the light distribution in a dense forest (01); the building's material palette echoes the forest colors (02)

below bottom I massing morphology and stacking diagram

traditional horizontal cabin configuration a
reorganization and consolidation b
vertically stacked cabin c

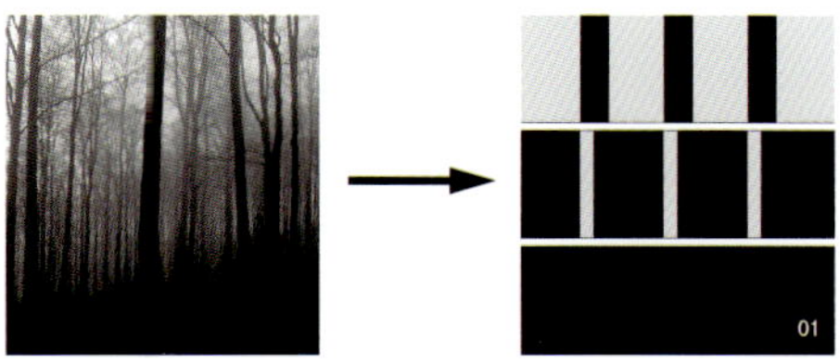

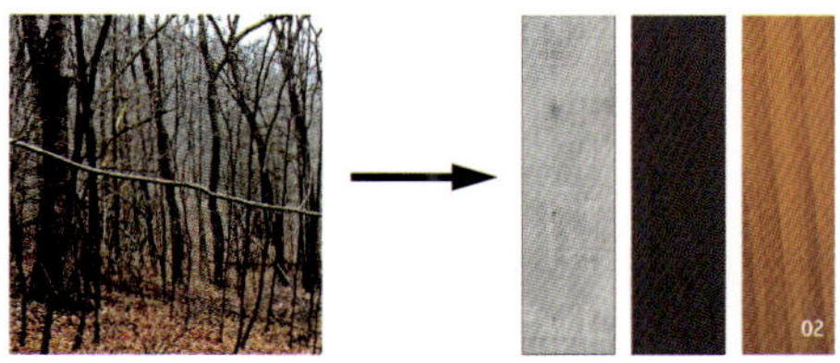

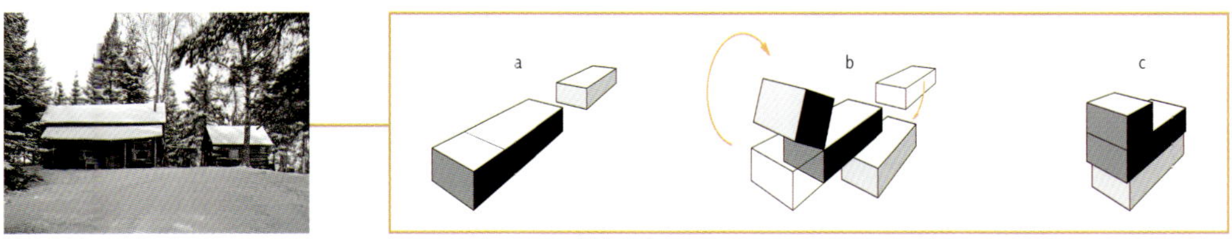

right I view from the plateau

center I facade studies: vertical base rhythm, opening edges, solid/void distribution

below I exploded axonometric; model views

01 clearing
02 slope and plateau
03 concrete base
04 entry
05 workshop enclosure
06 main floor plate
07 windows
08 cabin body
09 upper roof plate

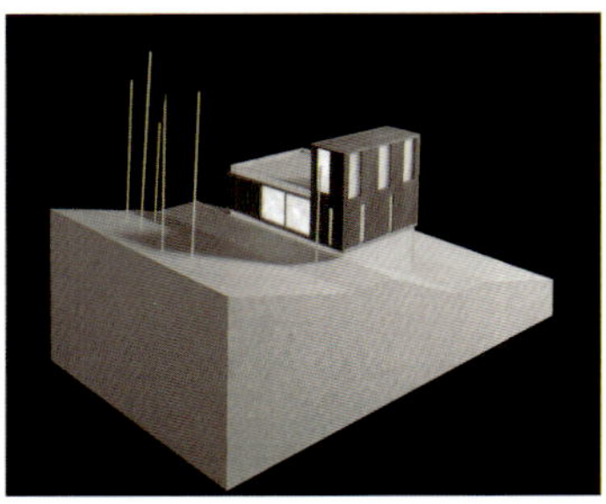

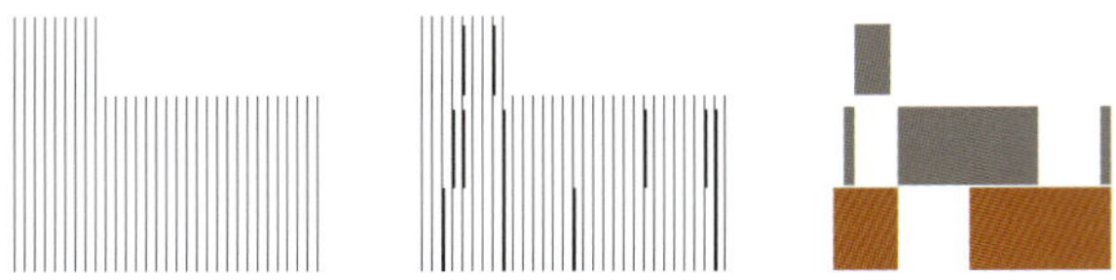

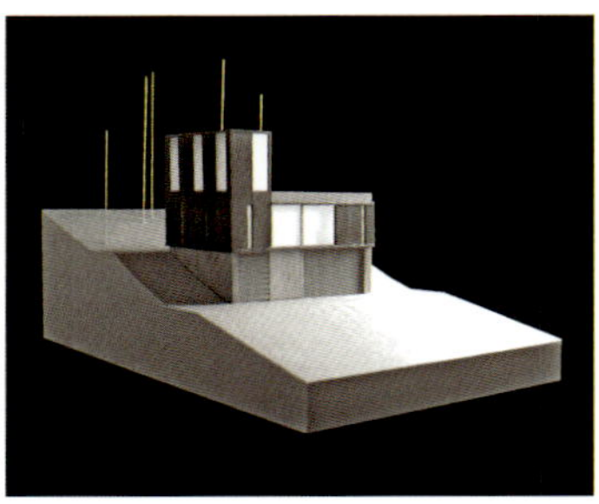

left I the hearth room connects to the plateau patio outside

below I strategy diagrams; floor plans

entry 01
washroom 02
closet 03
workshop I equipment 04
hearth room 05
galley kitchen 06
curtains 07
sleeping room 08
sleeping room 09
stove 10
plateau patio 11
observatory 12

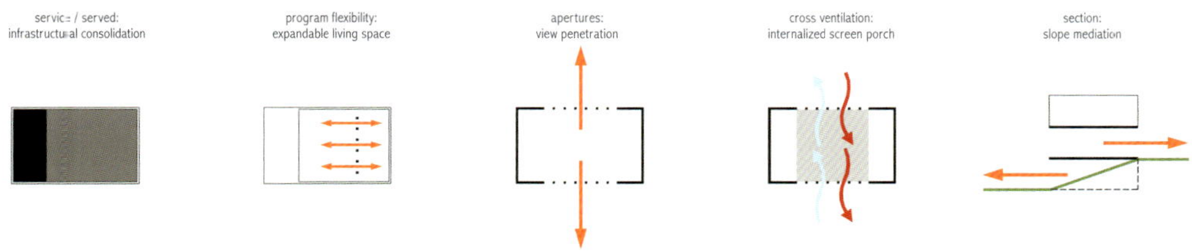

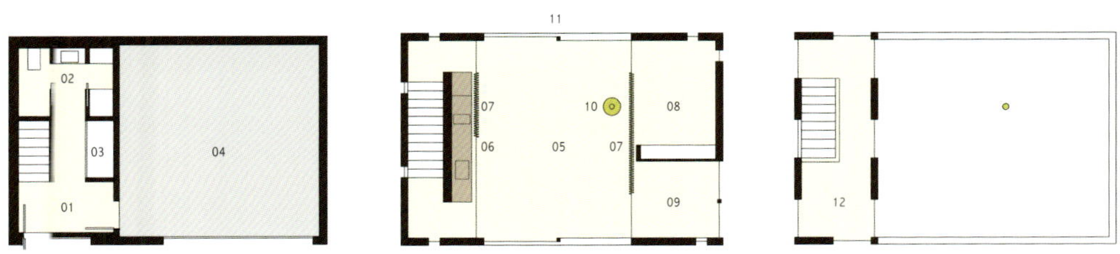

right I view into the hearth room from the outside

below I on the insight, curtains can be re-arranged, depending on the use of the space

LINEAR CABIN

St. Germain, Wisconsin

The Linear Cabin sits on a steep bluff overlooking Alma Lake in the sparsely populated Northwoods region of Wisconsin. A rugged gravel drive leads to a small clearing, where the simple bar building marks the threshold between the densely wooded plateau and the lake bluff beyond.

With its compact plan, restrained use of materials, and precise detailing, the Linear Cabin continues Wisconsin's rich legacy of cabin architecture—an unapologetically contemporary building that echoes the elegant clarity and rustic warmth of its typological predecessors while carefully avoiding bucolic sentimentality.

The cabin is composed of three identically sized, nearly opaque boxes separated by spatial voids, all tied together with a continuous, thin roof plane that spans the entire length of the building. The storage box offers space for canoes, tools, and logging equipment; the service box contains the cabin infrastructure, including entry, kitchen, bathroom, laundry, and boiler room; and the sleeping box houses two bunk rooms.

The void between storage and service boxes is unenclosed, framing views from the clearing toward the lake and offering a covered spot for a vehicle when needed. The void between service and sleeping boxes functions as the hearth room, the center of the cabin anchored by a wood-burning stove. The 15-foot-wide lift-slide glass doors bracketing the hearth room serve as picture frames, allowing for unobstructed views through the building from the outside and into the sylvan landscape from within.

right I the open-air void between storage box and service box can be used as a carport or covered porch

below I varnished cedar accentuates the continuous horizontal reveal between the opaque volumes and the thin roof plane above and turns into a vertical recess as the roof folds down

right I sequential massing model: the program is organized as three identical opaque boxes, pulled apart from one another

below I the hearth room occupies the void between the service box and the sleeping box

left I the continuous roof plane spans across the three program boxes and ties them together

below I floor plan

01 car port / covered porch
02 entry
03 galley kitchen
04 hearth room
05 stove
06 bunk room
07 bedroom
08 bathroom
09 laundry
10 boiler room
11 canoes / wood storage
12 bluff terrace

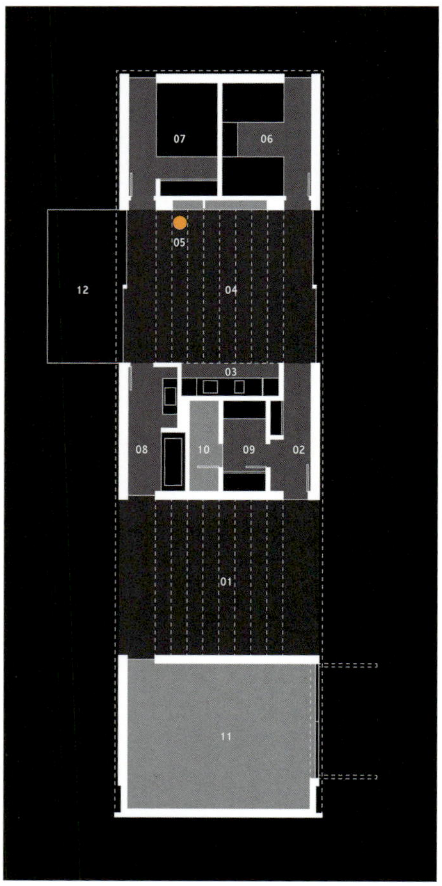

left I the large glass lift-slide doors of the the hearth room frame views of the landscape beyond

below I views of the entry area and the bunk room

right I walls and ceilings are clad in knotty pine that contrasts with the crisp, light-gray lacquered built-ins

below I entering the bedroom

BLOCK 27

Sacramento, California

Block 27 is a small four-unit apartment building in the Newton Booth District on Sacramento's east side. The compact structure sits on an empty infill lot at the threshold between an area of distribution centers, warehouses, and light-industrial buildings on one side, and a dense residential neighborhood with treelined streets on the other. In response to these two competing urban typologies, the project seeks to mediate between the large-scale, unadorned monoliths to the north and the fine-grained fabric of small bungalows and four-square homes lining 27th Street to the south.

The simple, three-story massing gives Block 27 a muscular street presence and echoes the geometric pragmatism of its bulky commercial neighbors, but unlike them, the building is not an obstinate, hermetic box. Instead, the subtle manipulation of its cubic form and the cadenced articulation of its envelope temper the building's volumetric rigor.

Stacked floor-to-ceiling wall panels in shades of gray alternate with tall apertures and faithfully delineate the building's entire perimeter. However, the wall panels' irregularity, tonal variegation, and random distribution, along with a large void carved out of the volume's top floor, intentionally subvert the purity of form for a more nuanced reading of the building—a counterpoint to the visual impermeability and stubborn self-containment of the nearby warehouses, allowing the building to transition comfortably from the volumetric heft of the commercial district to the more delicate scale of its residential neighbors.

Because of its convenient location next to Sacramento's major light rail corridor along R Street, which connects Newton Booth with downtown in a short commute, Block 27 does not offer enclosed parking for cars. Instead, the building provides shared storage space for bicycles and scooters inside a wood-clad volume that faces the street.

The wood volume articulates the building entry, its oblique side wall leading to the deeply recessed front door and into the vestibule. From here, stairs connect to the upper floors and terminate in the communal roof terrace, an outdoor living room accessible to all renters and their guests. Overlooking 27th Street and a neighborhood in transition, the roof terrace features a delicate overhead steel trellis and is tucked behind the continuous veil of variegated wall panels that clad the building, creating an airy outdoor room with ample shade and protection against strong winds.

The crisply detailed building envelope pairs cementitious stucco, wood, and glass. The exterior wood cladding extends to the inside and lines the walls of the staircase as it leads up to the communal roof terrace. A series of vertical lacquered metal channels and corresponding lighting strips complement the overall facade composition and its rhythmic complexity, their thin, bright yellow lines a subtle accent to the muted tones of the gray facade panels. At night, the vertical lights animate the building's exterior, giving Block 27 an unexpected visual presence on R Street as they radiate their faint, enigmatic incandescence into the neighborhood sky.

left I Block 27 is sandwiched between residential and commerical buildings

below I location map

right I view from 27th street

below I site and volumetric approach; unfolded facade organization diagram

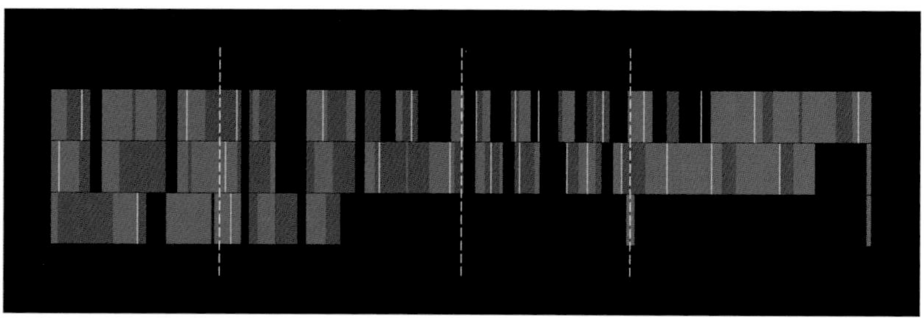

left I a series of thin vertical metal channels and corresponding lighting strips add to the rhythmic complexity of the building skin

below I floor plan and massing sequence diagram

covered entry 01
vestibule 02
bikes I storage 03
apartment 'a' 04
apartment 'b' 05
apartment 'c' 06
apartment 'd' 07
communal roof terrace 08

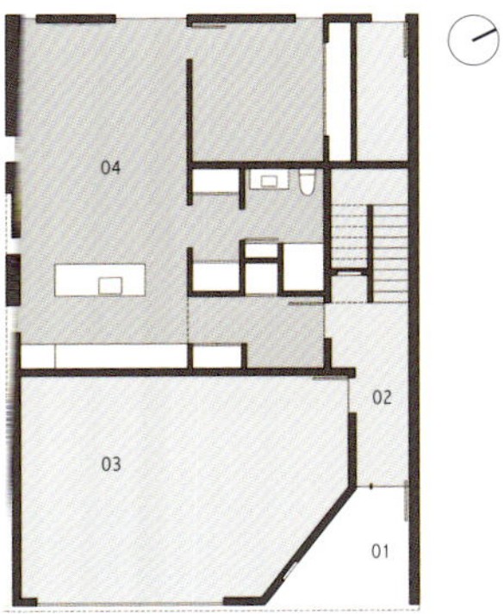

first floor

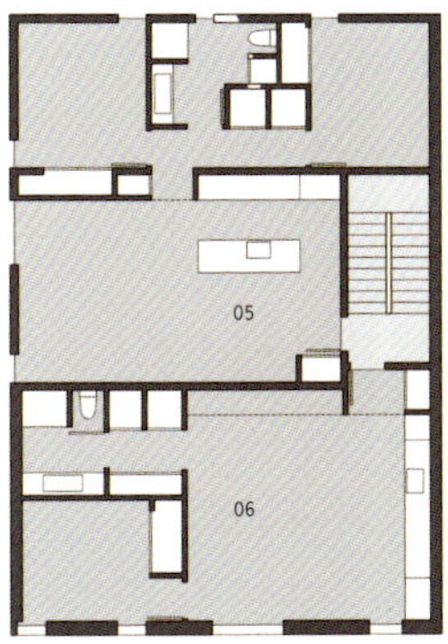

second floor

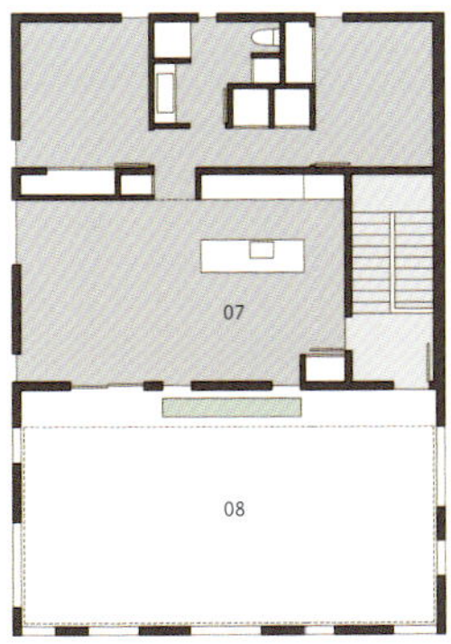

third floor

right I the communal terrace on the third floor is carved out of the building volume, making its mass visually permeable and reducing its perceived scale

below I building sections

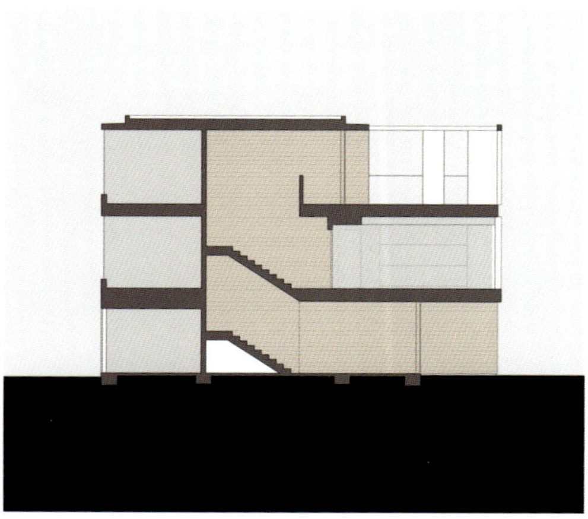

right I view of the open living space in apartment 'd'

below I the living space opens up to the communal roof terrace

TOPO HOUSE

Blue Mounds, Wisconsin

The Topo House was designed for a biomedical engineer and his wife, a sculptor and installation artist. After living for two decades in an old, converted church in downtown Madison, the couple, both avid cyclists, decided to relocate to the countryside to be closer to nature and have direct access to Wisconsin's expansive network of bike trails.

The building is surrounded by the unglaciated landscape of Wisconsin's "Driftless Region," an area with softly rolling hills and tight ravines. Based on early conceptual studies interpreting the site's distinct topography as a series of folded parallel planes, the house forms a low-slung, partially submerged volume with a meticulously detailed copper roof plane that slowly peels itself up from the ground and extends the adjacent fields as a green carpet over the lower portion of the house. The project demonstrates how a building can literally merge with its context, blurring the boundaries between landscape and architecture, between nature and tectonics.

The program is organized in two staggered bars with a total area of 3,300 square feet. Small exterior courtyards carved out of the building volume create an amorphous footprint whose ambiguous perimeter is normalized by the continuous copper roof ribbon. The roof gradually rises and ultimately

terminates in a dramatic cantilever over the large south-facing vista terrace. The courtyards—one covered, the other two open to the sky—function as sheltered outdoor rooms that provide protection against the area's strong and ever-changing winds. On the inside, rooms are interconnected to create a continuous spatial meander that traces the site's topography: the program is distributed on five individual floor plates, each one of them separated from the next by several steps, creating a progression through the house that leads from the entry at the lowest elevation to a small observatory at the top.

Echoing the dramatic surface deformations that occur when wind blows over the crops and grasses of the surrounding prairie, the building skin is composed of a high-performance ventilated rainscreen system with integrally colored concrete fiber panels, organized by 190 individually shaped, black-anodized aluminum fins of interrelated contracting and expanding shapes. Depending on the time of the day and the angle from which they are viewed, the fins create a constantly changing veil whose shifting geometry subverts the volumetric purity of the house itself. The rainscreen system is complemented by textured cast-in-place concrete walls whose deep, randomly spaced reveals juxtapose the consistent rhythm of the vertical fins.

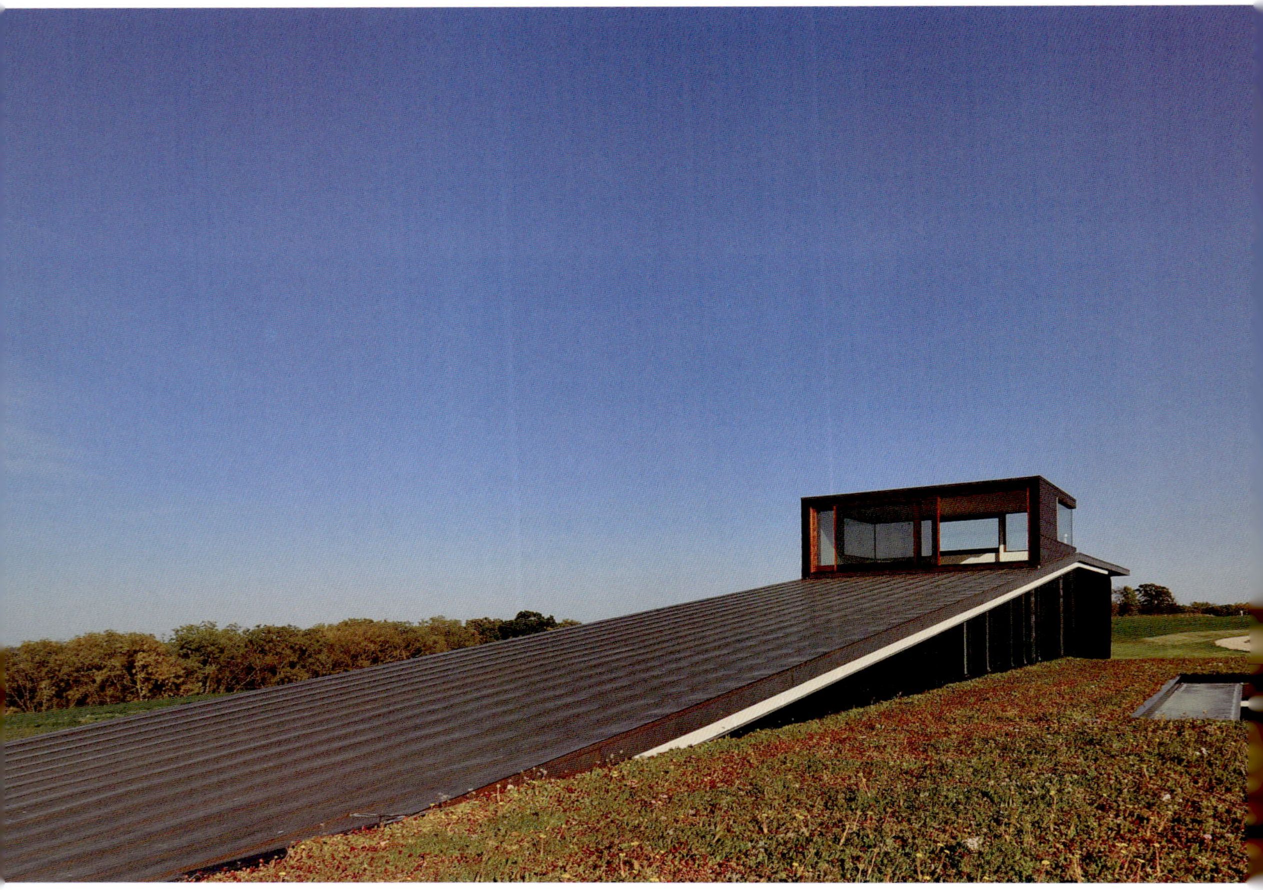

left I view from the lower green roof

below I site plan; conceptual model of the folding ground plane; regional topographic plaster model

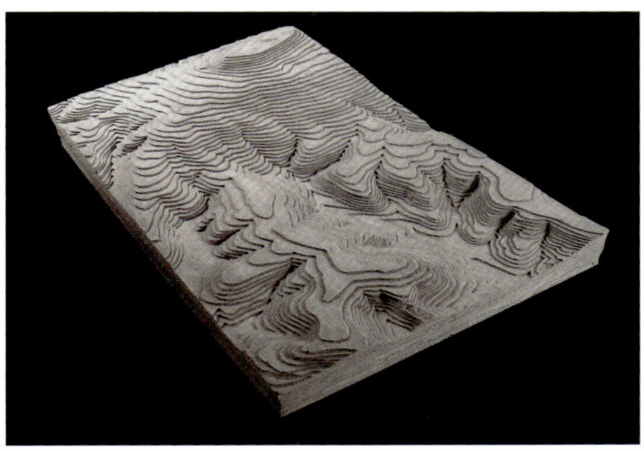

right I detailed section model illustrating the building's internal topography

below I the building form was developed in a series of study models at various scales and levels of precision

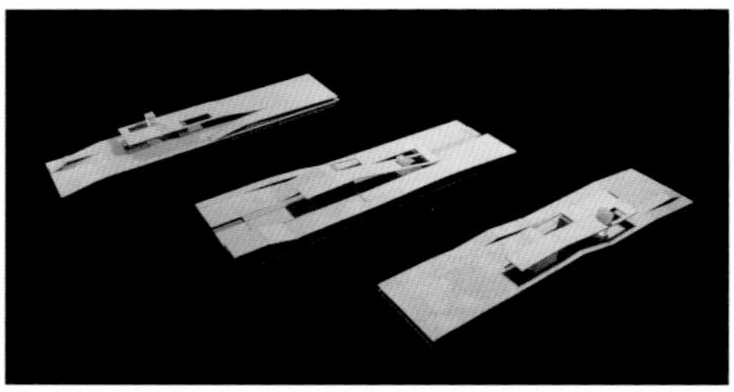

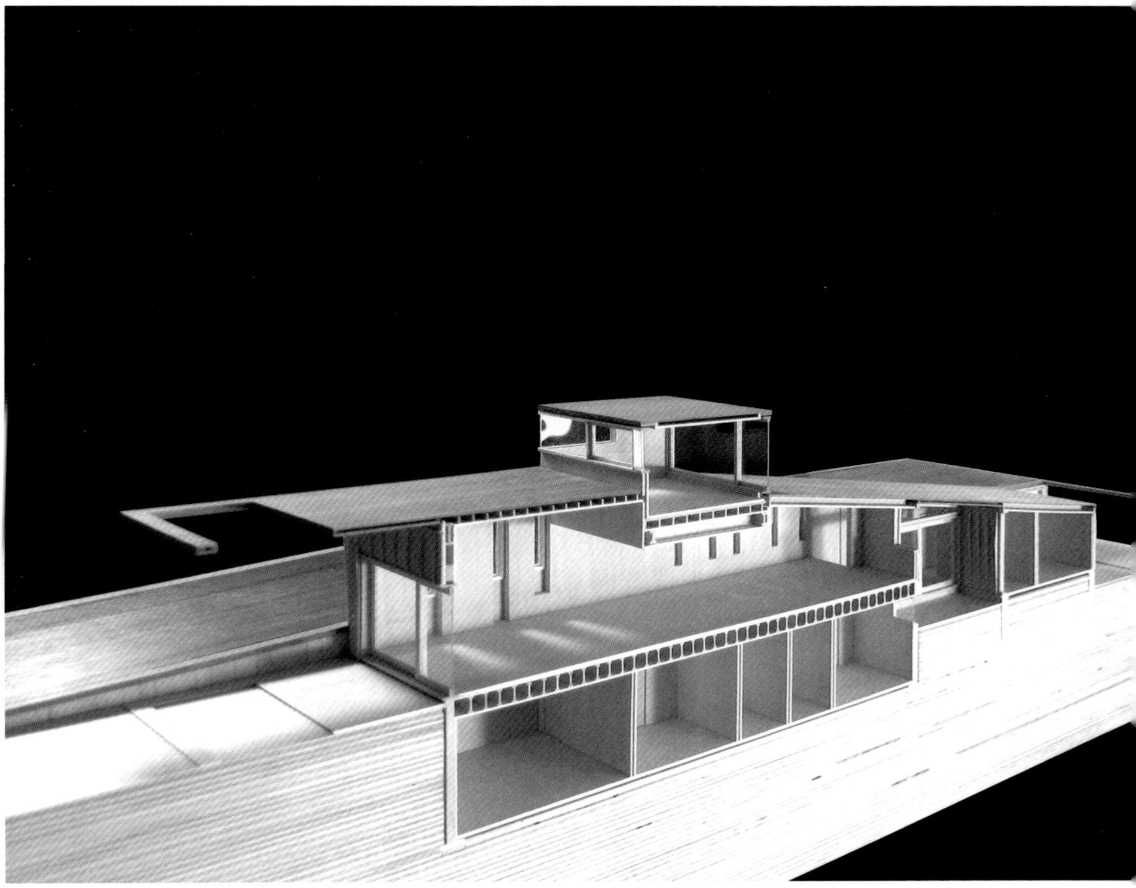

right I approaching the house from the southwest; the copper roof ribbon gently separates from the ground plane

below I exploded axonometric of principal building components

01 lower bar
02 upper bar
03 entry courtyard
04 garden courtyard
05 covered courtyard
06 vista terrace
07 aluminum fins
08 copper roof ribbon
09 vegetated roof plane
10 observatory

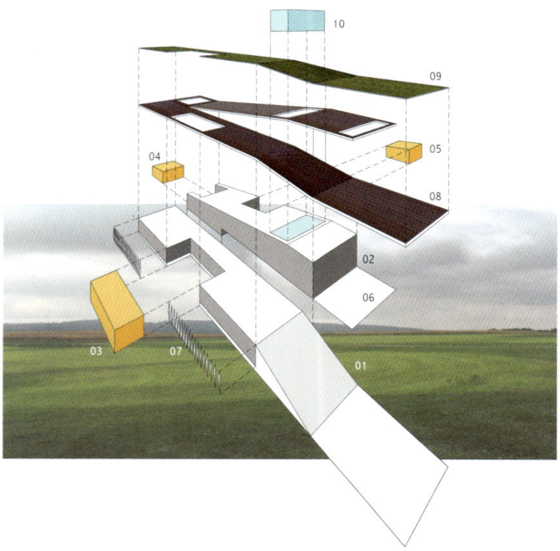

right I the entry courtyard leads to the oversized pivoted front door

below I floor plan and plan diagrams

01 entry courtyard
02 entry gallery
03 art studio
04 powder room
05 laundry
06 bathroom
07 closet
08 bedroom
09 flex room
10 kitchen
11 dining
12 living
13 vista terrace
14 covered courtyard
15 garden courtyard
16 observatory
17 garage

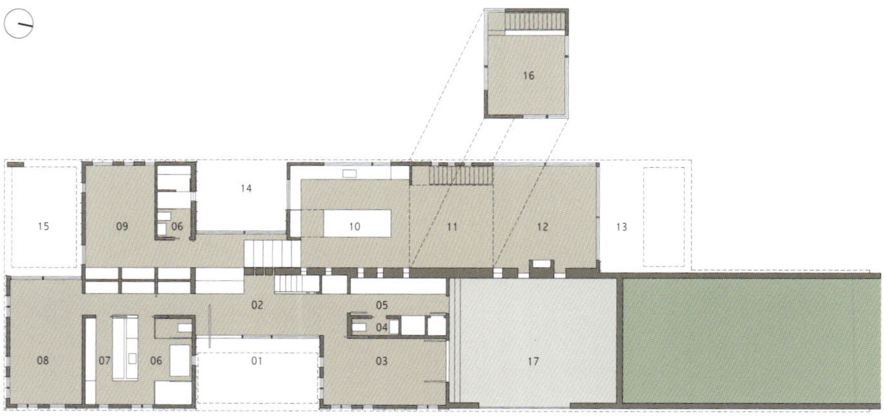

left | steps lead from the vestibule to the kitchen

below | the kitchen overlooks the living space, whose large-scale sliding doors connect to the vista terrace beyond

right I from the north, the house appears as a simple, low-profile volume

below I views of bedroom and bathroom

right I the restained exterior material palette includes
exposed in-situ concrete, copper, and black fiber-concrete panels

below I facade concept study models;
facade undulation diagrams

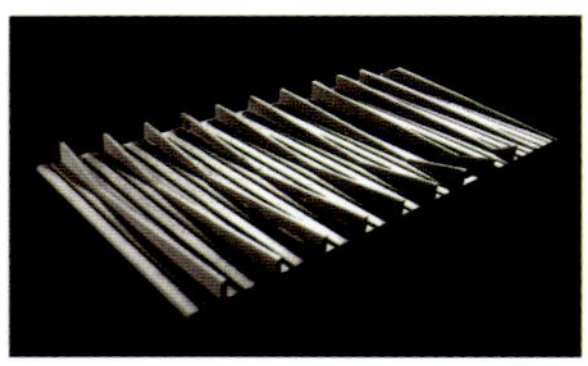

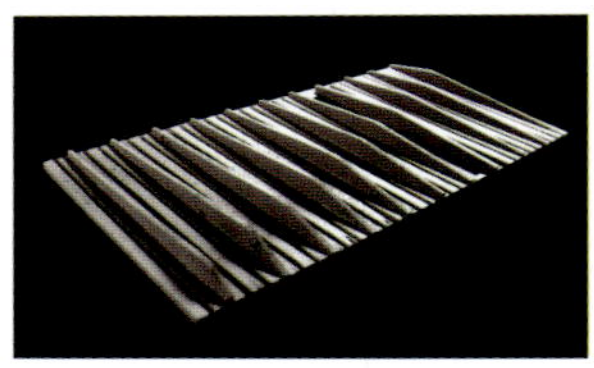

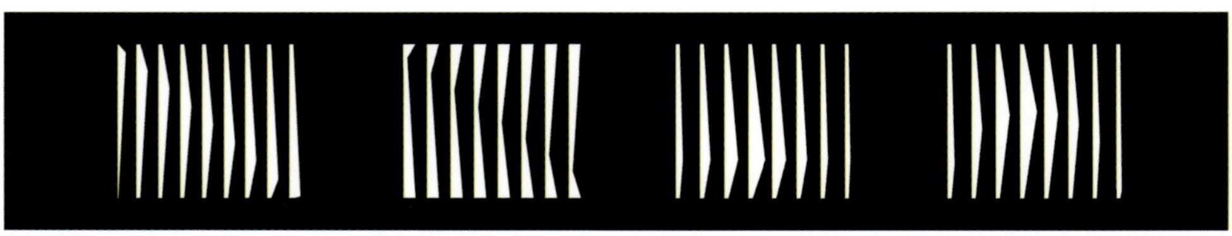

right I view in the evening

below I view of the south-facing vista terrace and its dramatic overhang; the changing shapes of the facade fins animate the facade in an echo of the surface deformations of wind-swept prairie fields

MANTEL ORTHO CLINIC

Cedarburg, Wisconsin

This small clinic in rural Wisconsin reinvents the exhausted typology of conventional medical office buildings and their introvert, fluorescent-lit ambience. Designed for a young orthodontist with a rapidly growing practice, the architecture embodies the very ethos of her own professional work—uncompromising purity, flawless efficiency, and rigorous precision.

Keeping a deliberately minimal profile, the building is composed of two complementary forms, their volumetric overlap visually moderating the perceived length of the building. The programmatic heart of the clinic, a spacious, open-bay operatory, occupies a light-gray volume that brackets a low-slung, dark-clad base volume housing the reception, waiting room, and other support spaces. A continuous roof perimeter beam embraces a grouping of exterior spaces carved out of the base volume—a trellised forecourt, a covered entry walk, and a small courtyard. A row of thin aluminum fins supports the roof plane and acts as a brise-soleil protecting the generously glazed entry area and waiting room from the harsh western sun. Along the street, the light-gray volume protrudes from the charcoal base and frames a long, striated green wall veiling the windowless laboratory. Analogous to the banded pattern of adjoining farm fields colored by their different crops, the green wall functions as an abstract billboard that gives the clinic an immediate presence, a deliberately artificial and somewhat wistful vestige of the area's vanishing agricultural past.

Inside, a wood-slatted ceiling plane cradles the reception and the adjacent, light-flooded waiting area. Optimized procedural flow strategies informed the clinic's overall program layout, with a central circulation spine leading to the five treatment stations in the open-bay operatory, a tall space with exposed roof beams and a glass curtainwall that frames generous views from the clinic's treatment areas into a small prairie meadow.

below | view from the west

Mantel
ORTHODONTICS

left I view from the southeast

below I palimpsestic location map with site and historic farm field patterns; massing model

Mantel
ORTHODONTICS

left I approaching the clinic from the parking lot

below I slender aluminum fins support
the roof and line the covered entry walk

left I the open bay operatory overlooks a grassy meadow

below I floor plan; volumetric morphology

covered path / courtyard 01
green wall 02
entry vestibule 03
reception 04
waiting room 05
consultation room 06
operatory 07
open bay operatories 08
sterilization 09
laboratory 10
office 11
break room 12
lockers 13
storage 14
brushing station 15
mechanical 16
restroom 17

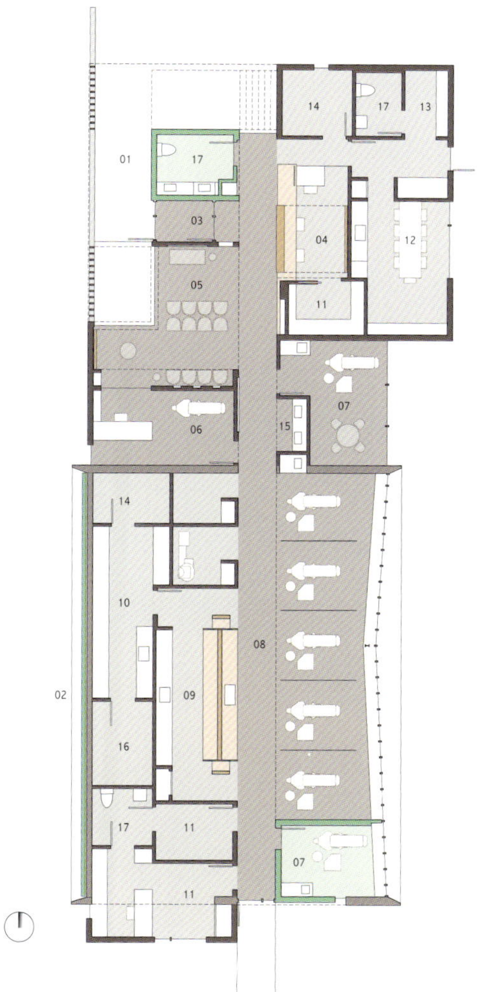

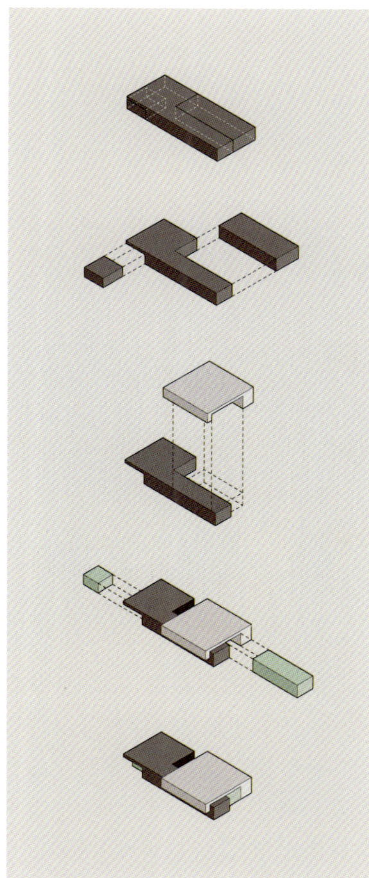

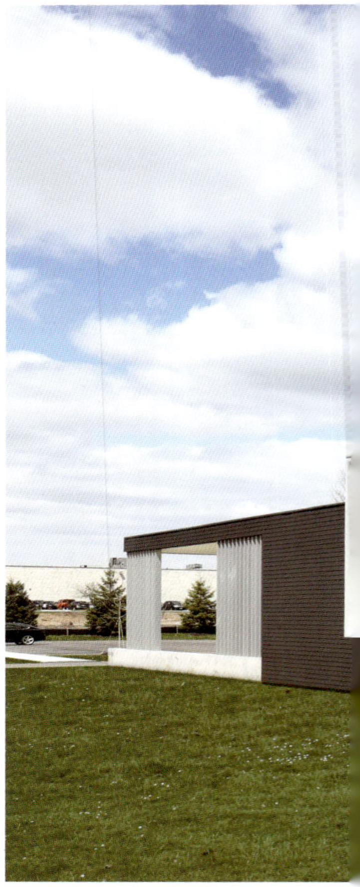

left I the striation and chromatic variegation of nearby farm fields inspired the compositional template for the facade

below I the green wall gives the building an iconic, site-specific appearance

right I a slatted wood ceiling articulates the reception area and extends over the wating room; a wall with vertical steel bars serves as the coat rack for patients

below I the bright waiting room overlooks a small courtyard

EXIT

right I in the evening hours, the building's inside reveals itself to the outside

center I workflow strategy diagram (plan view)

left I the tall glass wall in the open bay operatory washes the space in natural light

- doctors
- patients
- assistants
- admin
- back of house

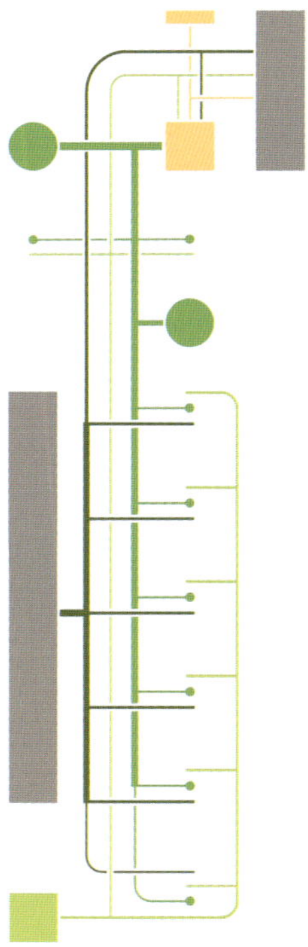

BROADWAY HOUSING

Sacramento, California

Broadway Housing is a dense urban infill development on an empty, L-shaped parcel in the southernmost part of Sacramento's Richmond Grove District. The 1960s construction of the Interstate Highway permanently severed the area from its historic core, leaving behind an urban limb with falling property values and a deteriorating social and economic fabric. After decades of neglect, the neighborhood has recently been rediscovered as an affordable and demographically diverse community with easy access to downtown Sacramento.

The project is structured as a dense cluster of nine single-family homes along Broadway and Yale Street. The design addresses the very different urban conditions and building typologies surrounding the site, negotiating between the loosely spaced, predominantly commercial structures on busy Broadway, and the dense, low-rise homes on quiet Yale Street.

The three homes on Broadway are three-story buildings, their height adding a robust urban presence to the currently fragmented street edge and taking advantage of the unobstructed southern views that the site affords. Sitting on ground-floor garage plinths, the main living spaces of the Broadway homes are elevated to the second and third floors to increase privacy and provide separation from the heavy vehicular traffic on Broadway. In contrast, the six two-story houses on Yale Street adopt the more modest scale and massing of the existing homes lining the residential street, their landscaped front yards and generously glazed elevations engaging and activating the sidewalk not unlike the traditional neighbors with their archetypal front porches and large living-room picture windows.

1015
1019
1023

right I elevated view, with the three-story broadway buildings in the foreground

below I site plan with unit layouts; section model

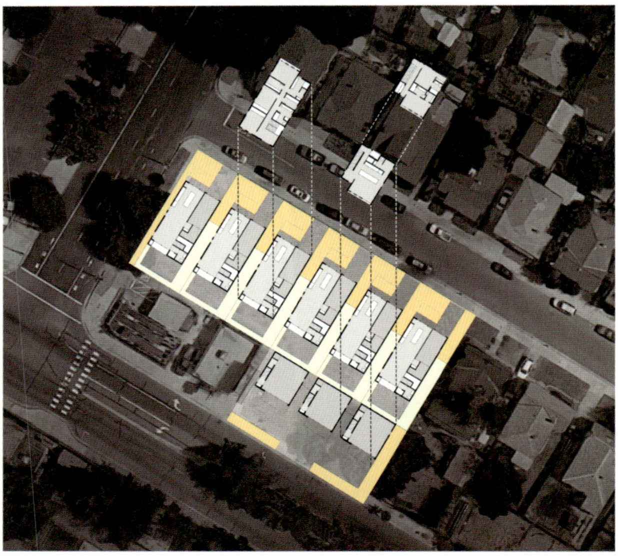

right I the broadway homes overlook a busy vehicular thoroughfare

below I massing morphology for the buildings on broadway (top) and yale street (bottom)

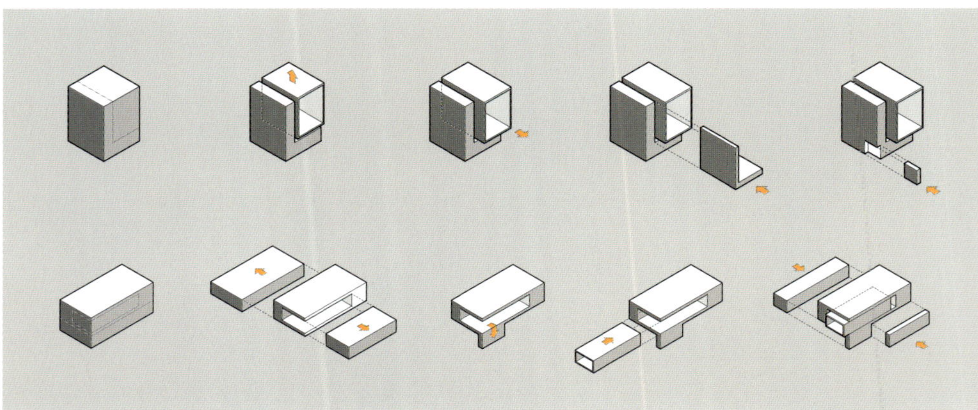

left | the living halls of the yale street homes are long, open spaces stretching from the street to the back yards

below | view of the buildings on yale street

left I the upper level cantilever
serves as a canopy for the front porch and entry door

below I vertical wood siding clads the cantilevered
volume and extends to the inside

right I the homes along broadway are inserted into a stretch of loosely spaced commercial buildings

below I the main living spaces of the broadway homes are elevated to the upper level

YOUR RESULTS.
YOUR WAY.
FREE Personalized Fitness Plans
24 HOUR FITNESS
001826
OUTFRONT
RUHKALA
MONUMENT COMPANY
Granite and Marble
Monuments and Markers
Bronze
Markers and Plaques
Historical Plaques and Signs
1001 Broadway, Sacramento, CA
916-441-2846

STUDIO FOR A COMPOSER

Spring Prairie, Wisconsin

An unassuming structure nestled into Wisconsin's bucolic landscape, this intimate retreat serves as a studio for a Country Western musician to write and record his music. A concrete podium, carved into a steep hill to provide storage space, supports a simple linear volume for the studio space, its long sides covered by a weathering steel shroud. Wall-to-wall glazed openings at each end of the studio provide access into the space and out onto the vegetated roof of the storage plinth, carefully framing views of the picturesque surroundings.

The steel shroud cantilevers over the edge of the studio volume to create a covered porch, a sheltered outdoor extension of the interior studio space. Along its edges, the shroud is slightly lifted off the concrete plinth, teasingly exposing a narrow, diaphanous clerestory that allows the studio volume to seemingly float above its base. During the day, the clerestory provides natural light for the storage space below; at night, it emits its soft, ominous gleam into the dark landscape.

The building materials—exposed concrete and steel, glass, and wood—were locally sourced and chosen for their ability to age gracefully over time. The steel envelope was detailed to exploit the inherent tensions between the strict modularity of the panel system and the ever-changing patterns of its oxidizing surface. Its warm color of ferrous corrosion echoes the hues of the derelict farm equipment left behind in the area's abandoned farm fields, turning the building skin into an ever-changing canvas. Alloy imperfections, surface oils, and roller marks from the steel mill all leave their individual traces as the material weathers, juxtaposing the building's strict geometry and formal restraint with a stubbornly unpredictable veneer.

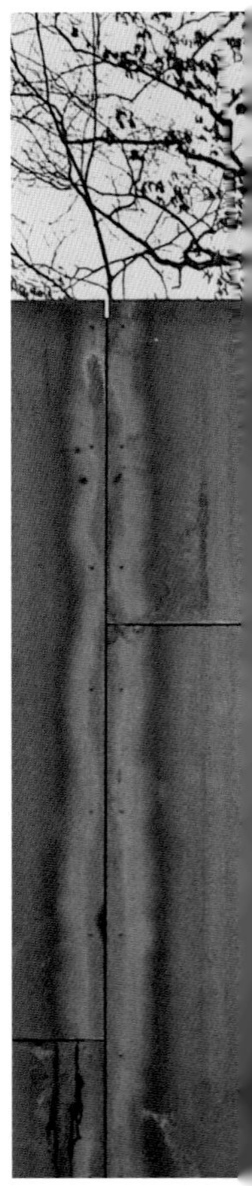

left I the building is composed of three simple components: a concrete base, a glass prism, and a steel shroud

center I site plan; farm equipment sits abandoned in a nearby field

below I approaching the studio from the north

left I the clerestory visually separates the concrete base from the studio volume

below I building sections

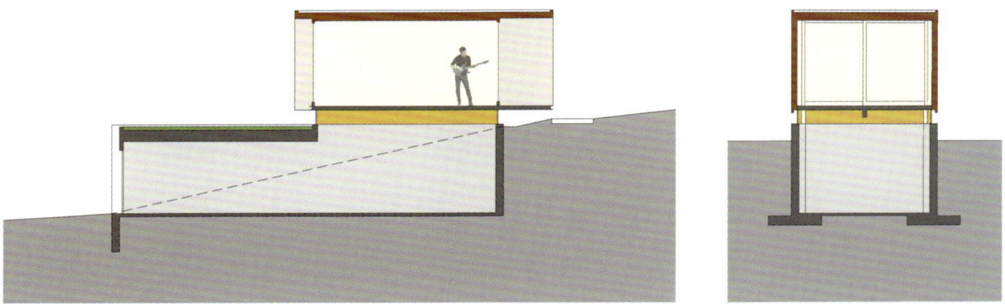

right I the steel shroud cantilevers over the studio space and functions as a covered porch

below I large glazed openings at both ends of the space provide access and frame views

right I detail view of the facade

below I the graphic juxtaposition of soundwaves and a steady metronome inspired the facade's interplay of visual irregularity and strict modularity

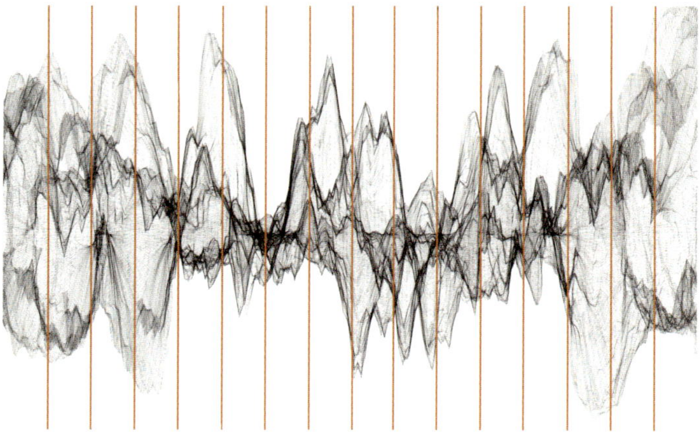

right I the musician steps out into the forest

below I exploded axonometric

01 concrete podium
02 structural steel frames
03 floor plate
04 weathering steel shroud
05 glass enclosure
06 clerestory
07 vegetated roof
08 storage access
09 terrain

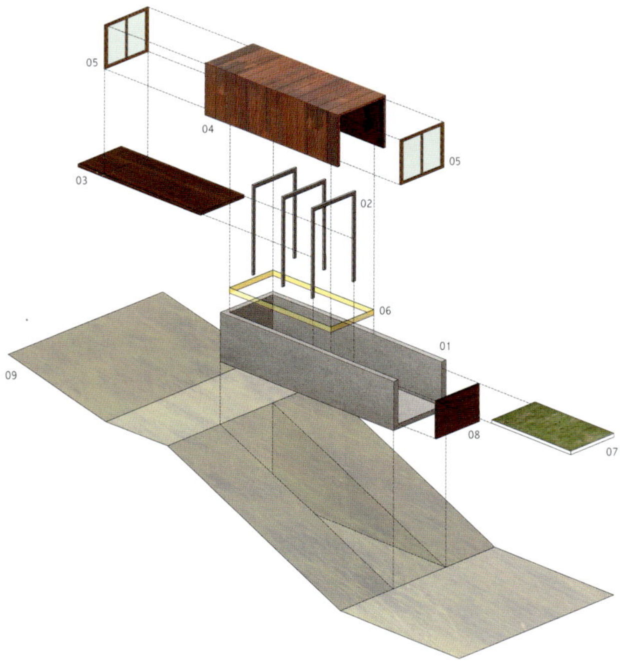

FLEX HOUSE

Sacramento, California

Flex House is an urban infill project occupying a long-vacant parcel bordered by an existing apartment building that marks the edge of Sacramento's Boulevard Park neighborhood—a historic district listed on the National Register—and a surface parking lot that serves nearby retail stores.

Designed primarily for a young family of four but purposefully planned to accommodate the ever-changing circumstances of life, the three-story Flex House pairs the family's main dwelling on the upper two floors with a separate but programmatically reciprocal ground-floor unit that offers adaptable space for residential or commercial uses. As a whole, the building with a floor area of 3,000 square feet is able to respond to future permutations in family composition, lifestyle preferences, and financial resources: the adaptable and fully accessible street-level unit can serve as the owner's professional office or leased to other commercial tenants; it can be converted into a "granny flat" for an elderly parent or transformed into a rentable apartment that generates supplemental income; it can serve as a guest suite for visiting adult children and their offspring, or even turned into a fully integrated, permanent expansion of the upper-level dwelling.

The building's correlative program is expressed in two complementary, interlocking forms. An L-shaped, steel-clad plinth contains the flexible first-floor unit and a tandem garage before rising up as a service spine alongside the slightly cantilevered, two-story wood box that houses the family residence. A continuous C-channel creates a deep horizontal reveal separating steel and wood volumes before transforming into tall, louvered apertures that accentuate the vertical separation between the two.

At the sidewalk, a series of slender columns and steel beams extend from the horizontal facade channel to form a trellised portico. From here, visitors can either access the main vestibule with stairs leading up to the two upper floors or pass through a perforated metal gate and proceed to a separate entry door into the ground-level flex space.

The organization of the main dwelling intentionally flips the conventional program distribution of two-story homes upside down, locating the living hall and kitchen at the very top of the building and the unit's three bedrooms on the floor below. The elevated vantage affords the living hall—the center of family life—unencumbered views of the city skyline. A linear roof terrace carved out of the two-story wood volume runs parallel to the living hall and functions as a shaded outdoor expansion of the interior spaces.

The plinth's subtly variegated black-oxide steel panels form a durable and visually arresting street-level building skin, its metallic robustness resonant of the neighboring commercial buildings to the west. In contrast, the family residence above is clad in vertical cedar, a deliberate reference to the clapboard siding of the historic homes to the east. The faceted perimeter of the two-story wood box is composed of a series of thick walls at varied lengths, their edges intermittently mitered to accentuate the building enclosure's extraordinary depth. Continuous, white-lacquered steel plates complement the wood facade and tie it together, setting up a network of thin strands that frame the individual wood walls horizontally and provide vertical datum lines as a static counterpoint to the shifting wall segments.

right I view from the street

below I location map; figure/ground plan of the site; elevated view of the building in context

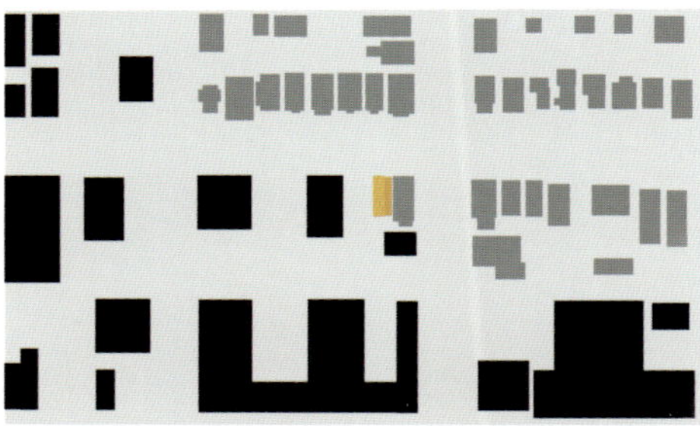

right I a trellised portico marks the entry

below I plan diagrams; floor plans

01 portico
02 entry vestibule
03 tandem garage
04 bike storage
05 bedroom I office
06 bathroom
07 kitchenette
08 living I work space
09 study
10 bedroom
11 laundry I storage
12 sitting room
13 powder room
14 kitchen
15 dining I living
16 roof terrace

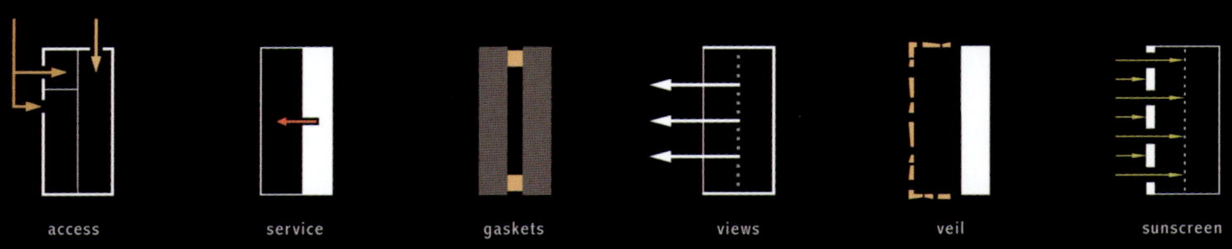

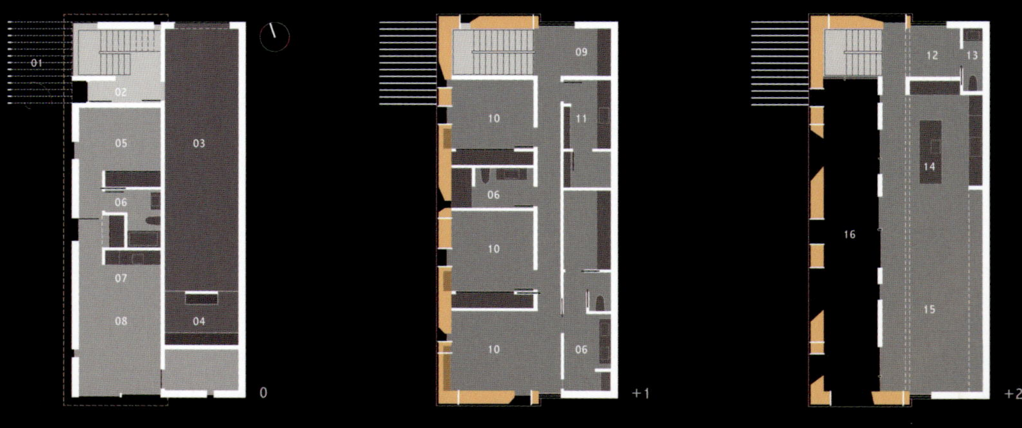

right I view from the west

below I sectional diagram: flex program scenarios and functional reciprocity; section model

A income generator
B home office
C family addition
D granny flat
E in-house caregiver
F guest suite

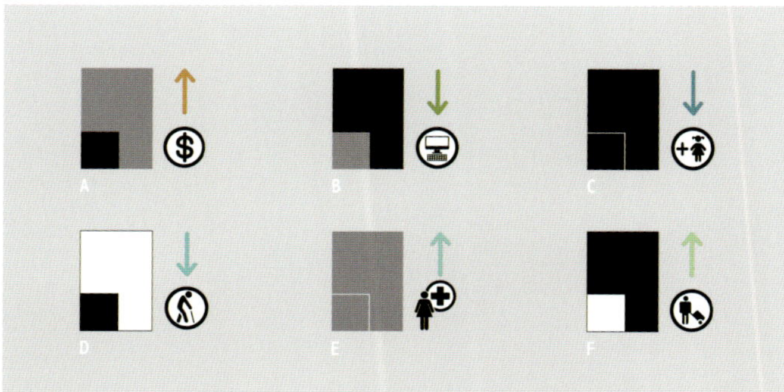

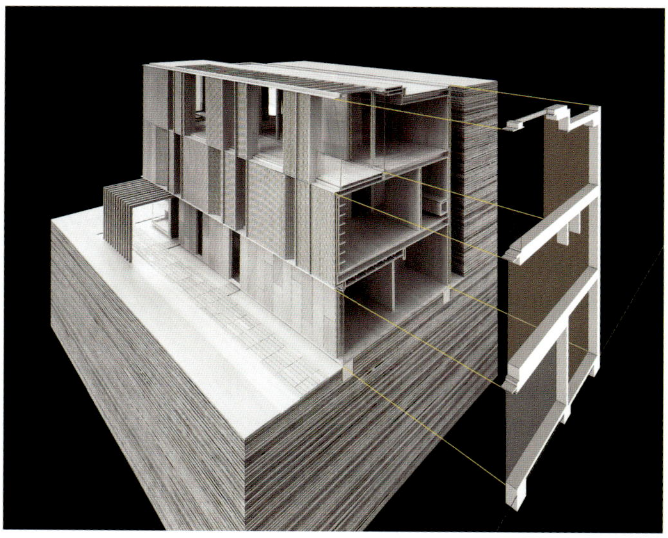

2020

left I elevated view of the third-floor roof terrace

below I the adaptable ground-level unit has access to the shared back yard and a small pool

right I the main unit's living hall spills out onto the long, shaded roof terrace

below I view from the back yard

left I kitchen, dining, and living are located on the top floor

below I the walls lining the roof terrace frame views and provide protection against the western sun; view of the living room

right I evening view

below I minimal, light-flooded stairs connect the building's three floors

SELECTED TIMELINE

01. PARTS HOUSE PAVILION, 2003
Merit Award, American Institute of Architects (WI), 2004
2006 Grand Award, Residential Architect Design Awards, 2006

02. HOUSE IN THE WOODS, 2004

03. CAMOUFLAGE HOUSE, 2006
Citation, American Wood Design Awards, 2009
Merit Award, Western Red Cedar Architectural Design Awards, 2009
Honor Award, American Institute of Architects (WI), 2007
Project of the Month, *Architectural Record*, 2007
Golden Award, Association of Licensed Architects, 2007
Project of the Year Award, *Residential Architect*, 2007
House of the Year Award, *Custom Home*, 2007

04. URBAN INFILL 01 (2004) and 02 (2006)
National Housing Design Award, American Institute of Architects, 2008
Honor Award, American Institute of Architects (WI), 2008
Grand Award, Residential Architect Design Awards, 2008
Golden Award, Association of Licensed Architects, 2007
National Housing Design Award, American Institute of Architects, 2005
Merit Award, American Institute of Architects (WI), 2005

05. FERROUS PARK ARTISTS COOP, 2006 (unbuilt)
Winner, Ferrous Park International Design Competition, 2006

06. THE BLATZ, 2007
29th Annual Interior Award, *Contract* magazine, 2008
National Small Project Honor Award, American Institute of Architects, 2009
Honor Award, American Institute of Architects (WI), 2007
Merit Award, Association of Licensed Architects, 2007

01

02

03

04

05

06

07. DOWNTOWN BAR, 2008
Record Interiors, *Architectural Record*, 2008
Honor Award, American Institute of Architects (WI), 2008
Gold Medal, Association of Licensed Architetcs, 2008

08. LAKE DELTON RESORT, 2008 (unbuilt)

09. FERROUS HOUSE, 2008
Honorable Mention, International Design Awards, 2011
National Housing Design Award, American Institute of Architects, 2010
National Small Project Honor Award, American Institute of Architects, 2009
Home of the Year Award, Custom Home Design Awards, 2009
Merit Award, Residential Architect Design Awards, 2009
Merit Award, American Institute of Architects (WI), 2008
Golden Award, Association of Licensed Architects, 2008

10. PALOMAR WELCOME CENTER, 2008
Honor Award, American Institute of Architect (WI), 2009

11. BLUR LOFT, 2009
Merit Award, American Institute of Architects (WI), 2009
Gold Award, *Milwaukee Home* magazine, 2009

12. SALVE STAFF CANTEEN, 2009
National Small Project Honor Award, American Institute of Architects, 2010
Merit Award, American Institute of Architect (WI), 2010

07

08

09

10

11

12

13. OS HOUSE, 2010
National Small Project Honor Award, American Institute of Architects, 2012
National AIA/COTE Top Ten Green Projects Award, 2011
National Housing Design Award, American Institute of Architects, 2011
Annual Design Review Award, *Architect* magazine, 2011
Merit Award, Residential Architect Design Awards, 2011
Merit Award, Custom Home Design Awards, 2011
Architype Review Award, 2011
Merit Award, American Institute of Architects (WI), 2010

14. LAYTON PAVILION, 2010
National Small Project Honor Award, American Institute of Architects, 2011
Honor Award, American Institute of Architects (WI), 2011

15. NEXUS HOUSE, 2012
National Small Project Honor Award, American Institute of Architects, 2013
Honor Award, American Institute of Architects (WI), 2014

16. REDACTION HOUSE, 2013
National Small Project Honor Award, American Institute of Architects, 2014
Honor Award, American Institute of Architects (WI), 2014
Honor Award, Residential Architect Design Awards, 2014

17. PROSPECT TOWER POOL PAVILIONS, 2015

18. NATIONAL WWI MEMORIAL, WASHINGTON D.C., 2015 (unbuilt)
Finalist, WWI Memorial International Design Competition, 2015

13

16

14

17

15

18

19. MOUNTAIN HOUSE, 2015
Merit Award, American Institute of Architects (WI), 2016

20. BAYSHORE DENTAL, 2016
AIA/AAH National Healthcare Design Award, 2017
Honor Award, American Institute of Architects (WI), 2017
Project of the Year Award, National Dental Office Design Competition, 2017
Design Innovation Award, National Dental Office Design Competition, 2017

21. SUTURE, 2017
Merit Award, American Institute of Architects (WI), 2018

22. BELAY MKE, 2017
American Architecture Award, 2018
Honor Award, American Institute of Architects (WI), 2017

23. D STREET HOUSING, 2018
Honor Award, American Institute of Architects (WI), 2020

24. PABST MANSION VISITOR CENTER, 2018 (unbuilt)

19

20

21

22

23

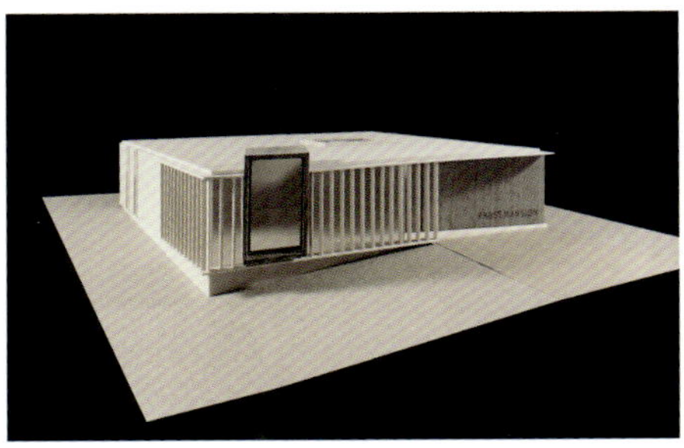
24

25. INDIE CAPITAL OFFICES, 2019

26. EGG HARBOR LODGE, 2019
Honor Award, American Institute of Architects (WI), 2020

27. ELM GROVE HOUSE, 2019

28. DOOR COUNTY HOUSE, 2020 (unbuilt)

29. ADVENTURE ROCK BOULDERING GYM, 2020

30. APW RESIDENCE, 2021

25

26

27

28

29

30

31. SPRING HARBOR HOUSE, 2021

32. CURTAIN HOUSE, 2021

33. FOX POINT HOUSE, 2021

34. 9TH & BROADWAY, 2021

35. POTHOLE PRAIRIE HOUSE, 2022

36. BURNETT WAY HOUSING, 2022

31

32

33

34

35

36

PROJECT CREDITS

KETTLE MORAINE HOUSE | **Location:** Campbellsport, Wisconsin **Completed:** 2020 **Project Team:** Brian Johnsen & Sebastian Schmaling, Eli Liebenow, Ben Penlesky, Angelina Torbica, Matt Wendorf **Structural Engineer:** CORE 4 Engineering **Contractor:** Rick Serwe Custom Carpentry **Publication:** *Dwell* (2020) **Photography:** John J. Macaulay

OAK PARK HOUSING | **Location:** Sacramento, California **Completed:** 2018 **Client:** Indie Capital **Project Team:** Brian Johnsen & Sebastian Schmaling, Andrew Cesarz, Ben Penlesky, Matt Wendorf **Structural Engineer:** CORE 4 Engineering **Contractor:** Indie Builds **Publications:** *Architect* (2018); *Architekt* (Austria, 2019); *Residential Design* (2019); *World Architecture Review* (2020) **Recognition:** National AIA Housing Design Award, 2019; American Architecture Award, 2018; HIVE 50 Innovation in Housing Award, 2018; AIA Honor Award (WI), 2018 **Photography:** John J. Macaulay

510 HOUSE | **Location:** Fox Point, Wisconsin **Completed:** 2016 **Project Team:** Brian Johnsen & Sebastian Schmaling, Ben Penlesky, P.J. Murrill, Matt Wendorf **Structural Engineer:** CORE 4 Engineering **Contractor:** JM Construction **Publications:** *Architectural Record* (2017); *M Magazine* (2018) **Recognition:** American Architecture Award, 2017; AIA Honor Award (WI), 2017 **Photography:** John J. Macaulay

PLEATED HOUSE | **Location:** Door County, Wisconsin **Completed:** 2014 **Project Team:** Brian Johnsen & Sebastian Schmaling, P.J. Murrill, Nick Woods **Structural Engineer:** CORE 4 Engineering **Contractor:** Tielens Construction **Publications:** *Architectural Record* (2015); *Residential Architect* (2015); *Home Designer & Architect* (UK, 2015); *Architecture Bois* (France, 2018) **Recognition:** American Architecture Award, 2016; National AIA Small Project Award, 2015; Winner, Marvin Architects Challenge; AIA Honor Award (WI), 2015; Residential Architect Design Award, 2015

ART GALLERY AND STUDIO | **Location:** Racine, Wisconsin **Completed:** 2019 **Client:** Robert Osborne and Vera Scekic **Project Team:** Brian Johnsen & Sebastian Schmaling, Andrew Cesarz, P.J. Murrill, Matt Wendorf **Structural Engineer:** CORE 4 Engineering **Contractor:** Bukacek Construction **Publications:** *Metropolis* (2019) **Recognition:** American Architecture Award, 2020; AIA Honor Award (WI), 2020 **Photography:** John J. Macaulay

LINEAR CABIN | **Location:** St. Germain, Wisconsin **Completed:** 2015 **Project Team:** Brian Johnsen & Sebastian Schmaling, Matt Wendorf **Structural Engineer:** CORE 4 Engineering **Contractor:** J&J Lee Construction **Publications:** *Architect* (2016); *Wood Design & Building* (2017); *Financial Times* (2017); *G&G* (Italy, 2019) **Recognition:** American Architecture Award, 2017; Merit Award, American Wood Design Awards, 2016; National AIA Small Project Award, 2016; AIA Honor Award (WI), 2016 **Photography:** John J. Macaulay

STACKED CABIN | **Location:** Muscoda, Wisconsin **Completed:** 2011 **Project Team:** Brian Johnsen & Sebastian Schmaling, Nick Woods **Structural Engineer:** Larson Engineering **Contractor:** Rick Hansen Builder **Publications:** *Architectural*

Record (2012); *Residential Architect* (2012); *OfARCH* (Italy, 2012); *Häuser* (Germany, 2012); *Designer & Designing* (China, 2013); *Design Diffusion* (Russia, 2014); *Financial Times* (2017) Recognition: National AIA Small Project Award, 2012; AIA Honor Award (WI), 2012; Residential Architect Design Award, 2012 Photography: John J. Macaulay

BLOCK 27 I Location: Sacramento, California Completed: 2020 Client: Indie Capital Project Team: Brian Johnsen & Sebastian Schmaling, Andrew Cesarz, P.J. Murrill, Ben Penlesky, Angelina Torbica, Matt Wendorf Structural Engineer: CORE 4 Engineering Contractor: Indie Builds Publication: *Architect* (2020) Photography: John J. Macaulay

TOPO HOUSE I Location: Blue Mounds, Wisconsin Completed: 2013 Project Team: Brian Johnsen & Sebastian Schmaling, Nick Woods Structural Engineer: Larson Engineering Contractor: Yahara Construction Publications: *Architectural Record* (2014); *Residential Architect* (2014); *Architects' Newspaper* (2014); a+a (China, 2014); *Dwell* (2015); *Umran* (Saudi Arabia, 2015); *H.O.M.E.* (Germany, 2015); *Casa Mea* (Romania, 2015) Recognition: American Architecture Award, 2015; National AIA Housing Award, 2014; National AIA Small Project Award, 2014; Residential Architect Design Award, Citation, 2014; AIA Honor Award (WI), 2013 Photography: Sitsrub Ognat, Bernd Fiedler

MANTEL ORTHO I Location: Cedarburg, Wisconsin Completed: 2020 Project Team: Brian Johnsen & Sebastian Schmaling, Ben Penlesky, P.J. Murrill, Angelina Torbica, Matt Wendorf Structural Engineer: CORE 4 Engineering Contractor: Peridot Construction Management Publication: *Architectural Record* (2021) Photography: John J. Macaulay

BROADWAY HOUSING I Location: Sacramento, California Completed: 2018 Client: Indie Capital Project Team: Brian Johnsen & Sebastian Schmaling, Andrew Cesarz, P.J. Murrill, Ben Penlesky, Matt Wendorf Structural Engineer: CORE 4 Engineering Contractor: Indie Capital Constructors Publications: *Architectural Record* (2019); *Archipendium* (2019); *World Architecture Review* (2020) Recognition: National AIA Housing Design Award, 2020; Honor Award, American Institute of Architects (WI), 2020 Photography: John J. Macaulay

STUDIO FOR A COMPOSER I Location: Spring Prairie, Wisconsin Completed: 2011 Project Team: Brian Johnsen & Sebastian Schmaling, Nick Woods Structural Engineer: Larson Engineering Contractor: Indie Capital Constructors Publications: *Architectural Record* (2011); *Azure* (2012); *Residential Architect* (2012); *Fine Homebuilding* (2013); *World Architecture Review* (2020) Recognition: National AIA Small Project Award, 2013; Metal Architecture Design Award, 2012; Honor Award, American Institute of Architects (WI), 2012; Finalist, AZ Awards, 2012; Merit, Residential Architect Design Awards, 2012; Merit, Custom Home Design Awards, 2012 Photography: John J. Macaulay

FLEX HOUSE I Location: Sacramento, California Completed: 2021 Client: Indie Capital Project Team: Brian Johnsen & Sebastian Schmaling, Andrew Cesarz, P.J. Murrill, Ben Penlesky Structural Engineer: CORE 4 Engineering Contractor: Indie Capital Constructors Recognition: RDAA, Citation, 2021 Photography: Justin Lee Lopez

ACKNOWLEDGMENTS

Johnsen Schmaling Architects I Staff 2003-2021 (*current):
*Andrew Cesarz, Garrett Grelle, Brodie Kerst, Eli Liebenow, Christopher Ludwig, Paul Mertz, Nick Moen, *P.J. Murrill, Patrick Osowski, *Ben Penlesky, *Amber Piacentine, Stephen Bruns, Taylor Thede, *Angelina Torbica, Erik Walsh, *Matt Wendorf, Marty Wicklund, Nick Woods, James Worker, Kelly Yuen.

We would like to thank our clients for their trust and open minds. Our work would not exist without the artistic talent and technical expertise of our dedicated staff, who help us translate abstract concepts into constructible reality. We owe gratitude to the many consultants and collaborators involved in the crafting of work, especially Matt Christianson from CORE 4 Engineering, the brilliant structural engineer for most of our projects, and to the contractors and artisans who turn our drawings into physical artifacts. We are particularly grateful to the following individuals: Whitney Gould, the late architectural critic who shared our early work with a wider audience, and James W. Shields, FAIA, who first made her aware of our fledgling practice; Karl Wallick, whose original idea for a monograph and his critical essay about our work in *World Architecture Review* inspired this book; former UWM-SARUP Dean Bob Greenstreet a well as Chairs James Wasley and Mo Zell, who have given us a platform to test our ideas in the academy; and Patti McNair and Megan Scott, both architects in their own rights, for their sacrifice, patience, and companionship.

Mountain House (2015)

ORO Editions
Publishers of Architecture, Art, and Design
Gordon Goff, Publisher

www.oroeditions.com
info@oroeditions.com

Published by ORO Editions

Author: Johnsen Schmaling Architects
Introduction: Clifford Pearson
Book Design: Johnsen Schmaling Architects
Managing Editor: Jake Anderson

10 9 8 7 6 5 4 3 2 1 First Edition

Library of Congress Control Number: 2021903483

ISBN: 978-1-954081-13-0

Color Separations and Printing: ORO Group Ltd.
Printed in China.

ORO Editions makes a continuous effort to minimize the overall carbon footprint of its publications. As part of this goal, ORO Editions, in association with Global ReLeaf, arranges to plant trees to replace those used in the manufacturing of the paper produced for its books. Global ReLeaf is an international campaign run by American Forests, one of the world's oldest nonprofit conservation organizations. Global ReLeaf is American Forests' education and action program that helps individuals, organizations, agencies, and corporations improve the local and global environment by planting and caring for trees.